# THE HISTORY OF
# ASHLEIGH ROAD
# – SOLIHULL –

# THE HISTORY OF ASHLEIGH ROAD
# – SOLIHULL –

Nigel Ian Cameron

BREWIN BOOKS

First published by
Brewin Books Ltd, 56 Alcester Road,
Studley, Warwickshire B80 7LG in 2002
www.brewinbooks.com

ISBN 1 85858 215 6

A Cataloguing in Publication Record
for this title is available from the British Library.

Typeset in Times
Printed in Great Britain by
Warwick Printing Company Limited.

# CONTENTS

# FOREWORD

In 1985 I was lucky enough to be at Edgbaston when David Gower scored his double century against the Australians. Led astray – of course – by my friends, the weekend celebrations of this wonderful innings continued unabated. On the following Monday morning, my dreadful hangover made me late for work and I therefore took what I thought might be a shorter cut through a road unknown to me.

The road was Ashleigh Road, and I spent nearly two hours wandering up and down in awe. By the time I got to the office I was doubly late. Richard Cobb – my boss – was in no mood for anything other than the best of excuses. 'Sorry I'm late, but I have discovered a road.' 'I didn't know we'd lost one', he replied.

It was agreed that I should research and present a case for Ashleigh Road to be designated a Conservation Area. That work was published as a booklet in November 1985, but not before I had nervously knocked at the door of the particularly special Number 14. I say 'nervously' because I was not sure of the response from the occupants to being 'conserved'. In fact, the response from Nigel and Angela Cameron was amazingly enthusiastic. Indeed, several months later they generously entertained the Birmingham Victorian Society and myself to tea on their lawns. It is fitting that such wonderful people live in such a wonderful house.

Now, some seventeen years later, Nigel Cameron has finished this book of which I was only able to plant the seed. He had drafted a history of No 14 which he showed to his neighbour. Ken Hewitt replied 'We have had much more interesting people living in our house, so why not write about ours as well – indeed you had better do the whole road while you are about it.' The result is this extraordinary work. A detailed architectural and social history of every single house in a road is quite unique. Therefore, I am humbled – but at the same time thrilled – to convey my utmost admiration of this truly remarkable achievement.

Furthermore, it is a worthy embellishment of David Gower's distinguished career!

*Simon Herrick, RIBA.*
*Conservation Architect for Solihull Council 1983-1986*
*19 June 2002*

# 1. INTRODUCTION

KELLY's DIRECTORY of WARWICKSHIRE was published at four yearly intervals and gave details of Solihull, including a list of its principal inhabitants. Ashleigh Road was not mentioned in the 1904 edition, but 25 heads of household (including Mrs Taylor of 'Bransford') were listed in 1908. The 1912 edition showed 33 (including 5 females). The 1920 edition was in fact published the following year. Telephone numbers were given in 1924 (9 out of 33 houses in Ashleigh Road had telephones), 1928 (13) and 1932 (24 out of 37). Up to 1928 only the house name was given (although Joseph Suckling's address was referred to simply as Ashleigh Road), and from 1932 only the house number. This occasioned some difficulty in tying numbers to names of houses, unless a family continued in residence across these two dates[1].

ELECTORAL ROLLS have normally been published annually, though during the 1920s there were two each year - in April & October. Apart from that period, a roll was current from October (based on a qualifying date the previous May), but since World War II they have run from February (with the qualifying month being October). Until 1918 only males over 21 years of age, who were qualified by occupation or property holding, were entitled to vote. There were several examples in Ashleigh Road where the wife owned the property but was not on the voters' list (for example the Cripwells at No 3 and the Stokes at No 20). From 1918 all males over 21 were listed and females over the age of 30. It was not until 1928 that the franchise for women was lowered to 21 years of age. Thus electoral rolls, whilst more informative than Kelly's Directories, do not list all adult residents until 1928. A roll provided the name of a minor in the year before he/she reached voting age, and since 1972 the birth date has been given. The age of majority was reduced from 21 to 18 in 1969. Apart from 1916-1919, Solihull Library has a complete set (on microfilm up until 1968 and in bound volumes from 1966). The rolls do contain errors, eg Narie Goode of No 19 was Maria Goode, and christian names have been transposed, eg Sydney Francis Crowley of No 35. An individual roll lists individuals in alphabetical order by ward. Ashleigh Road was originally in the Solihull ward (of the Tamworth Parliamentary Constituency), but since 1945 has been in the St Alphege ward of the town (in the Solihull Constituency). The list, especially from 1918 covers many pages (eg that for April 1925 covers 51 pages), from which individuals with an Ashleigh Road address have to be extracted: a time consuming process. Only since 1930 has Ashleigh Road been shown as an entity, with residents listed in the order in which their houses stand.

---

[1] *There are two houses which cannot be positively identified with any of the current numbers. Moniave, occupied by Walter Stuart Brown (who was also listed in the 1909 and 1910 electoral rolls); and Littlemore, occupied by Joshua Edward Cartwright, who never appeared on the electoral rolls. It is possible that Moniave was No 5, and that Littlemore was No 3. There is also Eastleigh in the 1921 Kelly which has not been positively identified.*

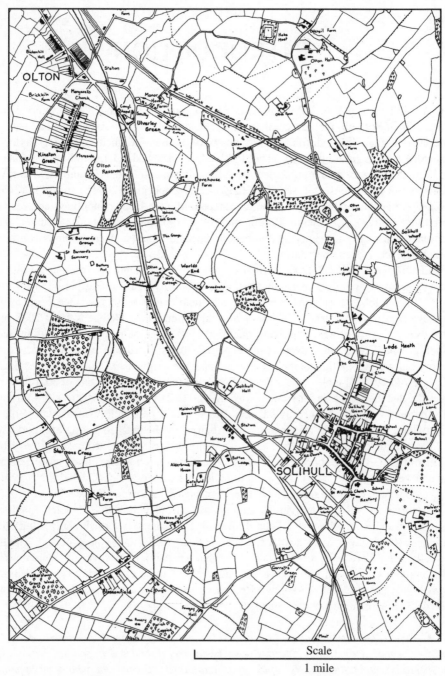

Scale

1 mile

*Map of Solihull in 1886, drawn by D.Moore in 1987. Taken from the 1st edition of the 6" Ordnance Survey Map.*

The NATIONAL TELEPHONE Company published a Midlands Directory in 1906, and a Birmingham & District Directory in 1908. Birmingham Central Library has copies of these together with those for 1911 & 1912. On 1 January 1912 The Post Office took over the National Telephone Co. Unfortunately the next telephone directory that the Birmingham library possesses is May 1930. There is then a run from 1932-1938. Continuous coverage starts at 1949. Telephone numbers in Solihull were one, two or three digit numbers to begin with; they were standardised to 4 digit numbers in 1931. Once the local telephone exchange had been converted from manual to automatic in the late 1920s, the number had to be prefixed by SOL, short for Solihull (telephone dials having both letters and numbers). The modern exchange number, 705, is SOL on the old dial. When occupation of a house changed, its telephone number often changed as well because, if the move were local, the leavers wished to take the number with them, or the incomers wished to bring theirs.

An invaluable source, where it is available, has been the HOUSE DEEDS. Conveyances provide not only the exact date when the ownership of a property changed hands and the sale price, but also the full names, occupations and addresses of both the vendor (not necessarily the occupant of the house) and the purchaser. Up until the 1920s a plan of the plot with dimensions was usually attached. Mortgage indentures showed the sum raised and interest payable. The money for the mortgage, at least in Ashleigh Road, was normally lent by two or three individuals (who always included a solicitor); only since the 1920s have banks &

Warwickshire County Record Office Ref: PH 372/2

*Solihull (or Silhill) Hall, dating from the 14th century and demolished in 1966, showing timbering. Ashleigh Road was built on fields originally belonging to this mediaeval manor.*

building societies been involved. Summarising the conveyances & mortgages for a property was an abstract (sometimes called an epitome): this often provided additional details by referring to dates of death, wills and executors. Several residents have been kind enough to lend me their house deeds, and I am most grateful.

The PROBATE INDEX OF WILLS has proved very useful. Besides the address of the deceased, date of death and size of the estate, this provides (until 1967) the name of the executors. Sometimes the occupation of the deceased is given and occasionally where he or she died. The size of the estate was given to the exact penny up until 1964, from when it was shown to the nearest pound. Since the late 1980s estates have been listed under broad ranges, for example 'not over £70,000' and 'not over £145,000'. Birmingham Central Library has the Index in books up to 1972. The Birmingham Probate Office has the Index from 1973 on microfilm.

The CENSUS each decade (particularly 1881 which, uniquely for the nineteenth century, is indexed nationally) has contributed to the background of certain residents, but the latest available to researchers is 1901, before Ashleigh Road was laid out. The burial records of St ALPHEGE CHURCH and several headstones in the Churchyard have provided useful information, as have certain headstones in Robin Hood Cemetery.

The INDEX of BIRTHS, MARRIAGES & DEATHS is maintained by the General Register Office (abbreviated to GRO hereinafter), and provides the quarter of the year in which the event took place. Quarter ending has been abbreviated to Q/E in the footnotes of the text. Thus, after a sometimes lengthy search, it is possible to put some details to names which have emerged from the directories, electoral rolls and house deeds.

I am grateful to SOLIHULL METROPOLITAN BOROUGH COUNCIL for allowing me to quote extensively from the Ashleigh Road Conservation Area booklet, written by Simon Herrick, which they published in 1985, and also from the Rural District Council minutes. The maps are reproduced, with permission, from the 1904 & 1917 editions of the ORDNANCE SURVEY. The WARWICK COUNTY RECORD OFFICE, BIRMINGHAM CENTRAL LIBRARY, and SOLIHULL LIBRARY were much appreciated sources of information and illustrations.

PERSONAL REMINISCENCES have been most useful. Accurate memories go back a surprisingly long way. Present & former residents of Ashleigh Road, and people who have never lived in the street, have provided much valuable information. I am particularly indebted to Anne Beal, David Blanchflower, Bill Dewbury, Sue & Ken Hewitt, Richard Ingrams, Pam Johnson, Ann & Roger Lucas, Diana Mitchell, David Patterson, George Pemberton, David Turnbull, Muriel Waters and Maureen Yardley.

I also owe a great debt to Joy Woodall who read an early version of the manuscript and made many constructive suggestions; to my wife Angela for writing the Historical Background chapter and finding the illustrations; and to Ken Hewitt for assistance with word processing and reading the text. I am grateful to Simon Herrick, the architect who undertook all the original research work to persuade the Council to declare Ashleigh Road a Conservation Area in 1985, for agreeing to write the Foreword to this book.

BOOKS written by local historians provided interesting information, and I have valued the following (in order of publication date):

*Solihull and its Church by Robert Pemberton (1905)*
*Solihull As It Was by Susan Bell, Joy Woodall & Mollie Varley (1980)*
*Paul Quinet by Doris Quinet (1982)*
*Ashleigh Road Conservation Area by Simon Herrick (1985)*
*The Roads of Solihull by Donovan Moore (1987)*
*Looking Back at Solihull by Joy Woodall & Mollie Varley (1987)*
*The Book of Greater Solihull by Joy Woodall (1990)*
*Solihull: A Pictorial History by Sue Bates (1991)*
*Solihull in Wartime 1939-45 by Solihull Libraries & Arts (1995)*
*Gazed at in Awe by Alan J.Sadler (1995)*
*A Solihull Century by Robin Jones (1997)*
*Travelling On by Edna G. Handley (1997)*
*Solihull in Old Photographs by Charles Lines (1998)*
*Images of England: Solihull by Sue Bates (1999)*
*Solihull & Its Villages by Joy Woodall (2000)*
*Memories of Solihull Village edited by Edna G. Handley (2000)*
*Solihull Past by Sue Bates (2001)*

# 2. HISTORICAL BACKGROUND

Solihull was laid out as a 'New Town' in the twelfth century, on the edge of the Manor of Ulverley, where it abutted the Manor of Longdon, and just off an ancient trackway which led out of Worcestershire and the salt workings of Droitwich, through the well wooded country known as Arden towards Coventry and Leicester. Plots were granted or let to craftsmen and tradesmen on burgage tenure. It grew quickly and its success was assured when in 1242 the King, Henry III, granted to William d'Odingsells, the Lord of the Manor, a weekly market and an annual fair on 18th, 19th and 20th April, the 'Vigil, Feast and Morrow of St.Alphege' to whom the church was dedicated. He had been an Archbishop of Canterbury, martyred by the Danes on 19th April 1012.

The church is at the top of a 'muddy' hill, ('sol' in Anglo-Saxon means mud, slough or wallowing place), 436 feet six inches above sea level. The underlying rock is the Triassic Keuper Marl, a mainly reddish mudstone with very few fossils which weathers to give a heavy, cold, clay soil, difficult to cultivate and naturally covered with deciduous forest of ash, hazel, oak and lime. However in much of the area the plateau-like higher ground is overlain by Pleistocene deposits of boulder clay, sands and gravels, with a sparser natural vegetation including birch and holly. Ice sheets and glaciers had moved across the area from the north and west bringing and mixing a variety of rock materials which was left in irregular masses as the ice melted, sometimes deposited in lakes dammed up between ice and hills, and generally dissected and redistributed by meltwater streams. The resulting soils are rather acid but lighter and better drained than the marls. They contain many smooth, water-worn pebbles of various colours and sizes, mainly quartzite in origin. The name of the field upon which the upper end of Ashleigh Road was built, Gravel Pit Close, suggests a larger deposit of gravel there. Such small pits were dug out by farmers for sand to help to break up the soil and for gravel to improve drainage or to put on roads.

Later rivers have cut down through the deposits. Solihull on the left bank of the River Blythe is close to one of the main watersheds of the British Isles. The Blythe drains northwards to join the Tame at Tamworth and continues on to the Trent, the Humber estuary and the North Sea. Only a few miles away, beyond Hockley Heath, streams drain to the south west, via the Arrow and Avon to the River Severn and the Bristol Channel. There is a great contrast between the Avon valley's lower, warmer, fertile and longer-cultivated area, traditionally called 'The Feldon' or 'open lands' and the well treed land of the plateau above, with its sharp rim, called Arden (from the Celtic 'ardu' meaning high and steep,) which had heavier soils and was difficult to clear and work and so was developed later.

In the Neolithic and Mesolithic periods, (10,000-2,400 BC), small patches of the lighter land would have been cleared, cultivated for a couple of years for barley and wheat and then left as waste. Herdsmen would have wandered with their cattle, sheep and pigs through the forest using temporary shelters, and hunters would have pursued the deer and perhaps wild boar. Early settlements would have been of small groups of families in clearings on the lighter, fluvio-glacial soils, above flood level but within reach of a stream for a water supply, and connected by a network of tracks, perhaps first followed by traders in tin, lead and salt. In the Bronze and Iron Ages more woodland was cleared, even the larger trees on the heavier soils, as farming developed. Larger groups of people, organised on tribal lines, established clearer boundaries and were prepared to defend them.

Arden was largely bypassed by the Romans who used Watling Street to the north, the older Fosse Way to the east and its branch, Ryknield Street to the west. Although there is little evidence of Roman occupation or influence in Solihull, they were about in the area and a few traces have been found such as some Romano-British pottery near Solihull Station. In the 5th century the Anglo-Saxons started arriving in Britain, some tribes advancing up the Severn valley and into the Felden; others spreading from East Anglia into the Midlands, via the Tame, who became known as Mercians or 'boundary people'. Under Penda the area was pagan but after his death in 655, Christianity, already established in the surrounding kingdom, quickly spread. In 669 St.Chad was appointed the bishop of the huge Mercian diocese and chose Lichfield for his seat ('cathedra'.) The diocese was too large and in 680 two new dioceses, centred on Worcester and Hereford and based on tribal boundaries, were carved out of it. Solihull remained in Lichfield Diocese until it was included in the newly founded Diocese of Birmingham in 1905.

It was not until the tenth century that Warwickshire was established with county boundaries. These remained almost the same until 1974. Until the Norman Conquest the manor of 'Ulverlei' was in 'Coleshelle Hundret' and so recorded in the Domesday Book but then these administrative units, able to supply 100 fighting men, were reorganised and Ulverley was included in the Hemlingford Hundred. Before the Norman Conquest the Manor of Ulverley was held by Edwin, Earl of Mercia, who had inherited the title from his father, Aelfgar, and grandfather Earl Leofric who with his wife, the Countess, Lady Godiva, is so well known in Coventry.

In 1066 all those who fought William at Hastings lost their lands. However, unlike most of the English landed people, Edwin did not fight at Hastings - he was in the North - and so he retained Ulverley. When he died in 1072 William gave it to Cristina, a princess of the Saxon Royal House, who also held manors at Arley and Long Itchington in Warwickshire and one at Bradwell in Oxfordshire. She was the sister of Edgar the Aetheling who had been the rightful heir after Harold's death, but was then very young and not crowned king.

Ulverley included eight hides of plough land (about one and a half square miles), twelve acres of meadow and extensive woodland. At that time it had twenty-nine families and a priest. Small farms developed, based on 'assarts', pieces of land acquired from the Lord of the Manor which were cleared, marked by hedges on banks and boundary ditches in many cases and sometimes developed into small hamlets of several families, linked by paths. Eleven moats, the sites of farms, have been located in the area dating from 1200 onwards. Elmdon, Bickinhill, and Longdon, which had common fields in the Hampton Lane, Yew Tree Lane and Marsh Lane areas and water meadows along the Blythe, had already begun as Anglo-Saxon settlements in the eighth and ninth centuries. The settlement at Ulverley itself, exact position unknown, was important to the manor until the de Limesi family founded Solihull on a better site for trading purposes where two roads crossed. Ulverley declined and became Olton, the 'old town'.

Following the Conquest, the track from the Black Country and the village of Birmingham to Warwick had become more important. The original way was down Church Hill, via Widney Manor Road to Hockley Heath and the Stratford Road, Lapworth, Rowington and Hatton. The new Warwick Road, which crossed the old saltway near the site of Solihull School and the river Blythe by a ford near Sandal's Bridge, came later.

In 1086, after the Survey was made, friendly relations with the Norman regime broke down. Cristina became a nun at Romsey Abbey and her brother went to Scotland or abroad, out of William's reach. Ulverley was given to the Norman family of de Limesi, first to Ralf de Limesi of Budbroke, near Hatton, and then to his great grandson John de Limesi. After his death about 1195 his wife held the property until 1198 when it was divided and de Limesi's sister Basilia acquired Ulverley. She married Hugh d'Oddingsells, a Flemish soldier who had been the leader of King John's Free Companions. In 1238 the property went to his younger son, William, whose large homestead was at Hob's Moat. He it was to whom was granted the market charter in 1242. His son, another William, held Ulverley from 1264 to 1295. It may have been he who started the building of Solihull Hall (more recently popularly known as 'Silhill Hall', see the maps) as a new Manor House, a typically mediaeval moated hall house. When he was killed in Ireland his property was divided between his four daughters. In 1319 Bishop Hotham of Ely bought it from John de Birmingham, grandson of William, but he was an absentee owner. It is possible that afterwards there was no resident Lord of the Manor.

Nationally the fourteenth century was marked by several bad harvests from 1312 leading on to famine in 1315-1317. The Black Death struck in Warwickshire in 1349 and plague came again in 1360, 1369 and 1374. With the loss of between a quarter and half of the population much land went out of cultivation and there was more cattle grazing. The town continued to trade quite well and the market continued but Solihull ceased to grow. Work on building a new, larger nave for the parish church which had started about 1250 was suspended, leaving the old church within the new outer walls; it was not finished until 1535. The manor eventually passed to the Crown in 1412 and under it had a succession of short term lords, some royal. From 1423 -1443 it was leased by Thomas Greswold, a member of the well known Solihull family commemorated in the Parish Church, many of whom emigrated to America in the seventeenth century. As he was a very successful lawyer in London he probably spent little time in Solihull. In the Tudor period Solihull Hall was 'modernised' by the insertion of ceilings and its division into smaller rooms. The manor was purchased from the Crown by the Throckmortons of Coughton in 1530.

In 1629 a survey showed Robert Middlemore to be a large landowner in Solihull. He had bought the 'Manor of Olton', but it might have been only the rights and titles but not the actual properties. He married Ann Greswold of Longdon Hall who was a co-heiress with her sister of the remaining Greswold lands in Solihull which may have included Solihull Hall. Solihull was by now just a small country town, surrounded by farms and patches of woodland, the seat of the local petty sessional court. The market had failed by the 1630's but one would still find here the apothecary, doctor, lawyer, inns and general tradesmen supplying the needs of the town and local rural area.

In 1717 the Manor was sold to Mr.Harry Gough. He died in 1751 and his wife in 1774 when it became part of the property of Captain Richard Gough. Like the other once important houses of Solihull, it had become just a farmhouse, the tenant being William Lowe. Captain Gough died in 1806 and his widow held the property until her death in 1835.

The fields around Solihull Hall were already marked out and named but it was during Mrs.Gough's tenure in 1819 that the Solihull Enclosure Act was passed, the remaining wasteland in the area enclosed and about 40 old lanes and tracks closed. (There is no suggestion that Ashleigh Road follows the line of any of them.) When Mrs.Gough died in 1835 Solihull Hall and its farmlands were bought by Thomas Chattock (1774-1844) of Silhill House. This was also a farm, on the corner of Station Road and Poplar Road, on the site of the Swan Inn mentioned in 1583. It was demolished in 1926. In 1840 the tenant of the Hall was William Grove, the area being about 143 acres.

The Chattock family came from Castle Bromwich but Thomas was already known in Solihull, having in 1798 signed an association for the defence of the Town and Parish of Solihull by raising a Troop of Horse numbering 50 or upward (which would not go abroad) and been nominated as their Lieutenant. By the 1840's Thomas owned about a quarter of the land in Solihull parish. In 1844 his land passed to his son, the Attorney Henry Harvey Chattock (1819-1898.) He refused to sell any land to Charles Lines' father, saying, "We've never sold any land yet and I don't suppose we ever shall. You can have some on a lease but you mustn't put any engine on it."

It was Thomas' youngest son Richard, (born 1825), an artist and photographer of Northmede Cottage, (on Station Road, facing the old St.Martin's School,) who inherited the land in 1898 and in 1903 sold the fields on which Ashleigh Road was built. Solihull Hall was illegally demolished in March 1966 by its owner Malcolm Ross, a property developer, who was subsequently fined the then maximum sum of £100, and ordered to pay £84 costs. Its remains *were removed to the nearby airport and there interred .... an irreparable loss to Solihull.* (Charles Lines).

# 3. THE DEVELOPMENT
# OF ASHLEIGH ROAD

Ashleigh Road connected the main Birmingham-Warwick Road to the original Solihull Station, which had been built when Brunel's wide gauge railway line from Birmingham to Paddington opened in 1852. The line was converted to standard gauge in 1869, the year Olton Station was opened. With the rapid growth of Birmingham in the last decades of the 19th century, people who had prospered moved out of the city and Solihull - 7 miles distant - began to grow. Ashleigh Road was in an excellent location.

In 1861 the population of the village was about 1500, and of the 12,365 acre parish as a whole was 3329[1]. The figures were very similar to what they had been in 1841. Growth at 20 year intervals was then as follows:

| Date | Estimated Population of Solihull Village | Population of Solihull Parish |
|------|------------------------------------------|------------------------------|
| 1861 | 1,500 | 3,329 |
| 1881 | 1,600 | 4,510 |
| 1901 | 3,700 | 7,517 |
| 1921 | 6,000 | 11,552 |

To cope with these increases local government also developed. Under the Public Health Act of 1872 the Board of Guardians, which had been created in 1836 to oversee the welfare of the poor, became the Solihull Rural Sanitary Authority, adding drainage & sewerage to its responsibilities. The Authority met fortnightly, dealing with matters relating to the poor in the morning and with public health in the afternoon. Under the Local Government Act of 1894 the Sanitary Authority was replaced by the Solihull Rural District Council, with 18 members responsible for the affairs of 11 parishes. It immediately established a sophisticated administration with standing committees for finance, allotments, sanitary & public works, education, general purposes & health. Several officers were appointed: a part-time Clerk (£137-10s pa), a shared Medical Officer, and a Surveyor (£175). The latter, Mr A.E.Currall later had 2 assistants - a Treasurer & an Inspector of Nuisances. RDC meetings were held in the boardroom of Solihull workhouse (on the site of the present hospital). About 1905 a permanent council office was established in Streetsbrook Road (where the fire station is now), with a depot and two cottages: one for the Clerk and the other for the Surveyor. In 1932 Solihull became an Urban District Council covering 20,365 acres and a population of 25,373. In 1954 it became a Municipal Borough; in 1964 a County Borough

---

[1] *1861 Census*

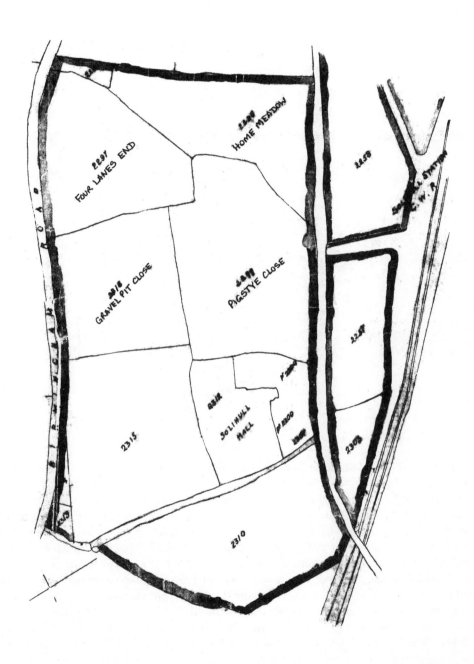

*Field plan of the lands around Solihull Hall, (from the Deeds of No 3 Ashleigh Road.)*

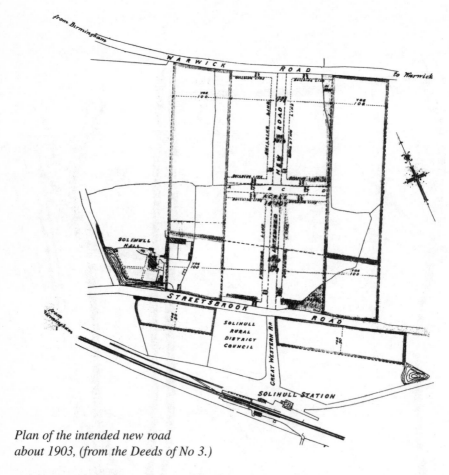

*Plan of the intended new road*
*about 1903, (from the Deeds of No 3.)*

(Luton was upgraded at the same time - the first since Doncaster in 1926); and in 1974 a Metropolitan Borough.

Ashleigh Road was constructed in 1903/4 on some of the fields to the east of Solihull Hall. Henry Harvey Chattock had died on 2 November 1898 leaving the bulk of his estate[2] to his brother Richard Samuel Chattock JP. The estate included Solihull Hall and the land surrounding it, which their father Thomas Chattock (died 22 July 1844) had purchased in 1834[3]. Richard Chattock decided to sell a rectangle of land between the Warwick & Streetsbrook Roads, 390 yards long, with a width of 175 yards. The centre point of the latter dimension was exactly opposite Great Western Road, the approach from Streetsbrook Road to Solihull Station. This area covered two fields - Gravel Pit Close, arable (the 1886 Ordnance Survey map reference was 2316) & Pigstye Close, pasture (2299) - and small parts of two other fields - Four Lanes End, arable (2297) & Home Meadow, pasture (2298). The descriptive use

---

[2] *Listed as £79,842-9-3d in the Probate Index of Wills. This is worth about £5m at 2000 prices.*
[3] *Information from the Deeds of No 3 Ashleigh Road.*

*Warwickshire County Record Office Ref: PH 352/164/19*

*Ashleigh Road from a postcard posted on 28th September 1905 showing, on the right, Nos 25 and 23 with walls and gates, the fenced gap where The Crescent would be built, No 21 and the handed pairs, 17/15, 13/11 and 9/7. On the left only Nos 22 and 14 are complete. Note the gravel road and footpaths and newly planted lime trees.*

of the fields came from a letter dated 16 March 1904 from the Estate Duty Office of Somerset House to Messrs Dunn & Duncan, solicitors. In all it amounted to 14.107 acres, and the Conveyance to Joseph Albert Wells dated 10 March 1903 stated the price as £3,526-15-0d.

Mr Wells was described in that document as a contractor of Birmingham, but in 1913 when mortgaging No 3 Ashleigh Road he was a butcher of Newton Row, Birmingham and by 1920, when selling that property, he had moved to Manchester Street - with no occupation given. Basically a butcher, Joseph Wells does not appear to have been a building contractor and today we would call him a developer.

Under the terms of the Conveyance Mr Wells was obliged to;

*Erect a good & substantial fence no less than 5ft or more than 7ft high on the east & west boundaries.*

*Within two years construct a road between Warwick & Streetsbrook Roads to Solihull District Council specifications, and to keep such a road in repair until taken over by the District Council. Until that occurred the purchaser was at liberty to fix a gate at each end of the road and to keep the same locked during such times as he might think desirable: the vendor, his servants and all other persons authorised to use the road being provided with keys. The vendor & his servants to have full right to pass at all times by day or night with or without horses, carts, carriages, wagons, traction engines & motor cars, and to drive cattle, sheep or other animals.*

*Permit the vendor to connect any road he might wish to make across the centre of the plot, and to connect with the sewers, gas & water pipes that would be constructed on the land conveyed.*

Warwickshire County Record Office Ref: PH 372/4

*Solihull Station about 1908. Opened in 1852, it had recently been extended. A signal box and footbridge were erected to accommodate heavier traffic and increasing numbers of commuters travelling to Birmingham.*

*Not permit anything that might grow to be a nuisance, disturbance or annoyance to the vendor, or which might depreciate the value of the vendor's estate.*

*Not erect any building other than private dwelling houses, detched or semi-detached (with stables, offices & outbuildings, greenhouses, vineries, summer houses, potting sheds, bicycle houses & fowl pens). Nor erect hoardings for advertisements except those relating to the selling or letting of the properties.*

*No detached house lying to the north of the cross road was allowed to cost less than £600 (exclusive of stables, offices & outbuildings) nor pair of semi-detached houses less than £1200 (ditto). South of the cross road the figures were £500 & £900 respectively.*

*No building was to be erected within 30ft of any road.*

It was soon realised that the space allowed for the cross road was not wide enough, so a further Indenture dated 10 July 1903 widened the gap on its south side.

Joseph Wells wasted no time in constructing the road between the Warwick & Streetsbrook Roads. It is believed his contractor was Trentham of Cowhayes[4]. The Ordnance Survey of 1904 indicated Ashleigh Road in dotted lines with an 80 yard development boundary either side, but no plots yet defined. In Kelly's Directory for 1904 there was no mention of Ashleigh Road. In fact several houses were already in course of building, as the Solihull Rural District Council minutes of 15 March 1904 made clear. At that meeting the Surveyor recommended that '*the sewer in Birmingham Road* (now Warwick Road) *be extended for about 20 yards to take sewage from houses now in course of erection in*

---

[4] *Information from Mr Bill Dewbury*

*Ashleigh Road about 1910, from the north. Note the gravel road, the walls and gates of No 1 on the left. The garden of No 2 on the right is not yet fenced. It was possibly not occupied until 1914.*

*Ashleigh Road'*. This was agreed at an estimated cost of £15. The reason for the naming of the street as Ashleigh Road has not yet been discovered.

At the Solihull Rural District Council Meeting on 14 March 1905, the Surveyor submitted a letter from Messrs Rowlands & Co (Joseph Wells' solicitors) dated 13 January asking the Council to take over Ashleigh Road and declare it to be a public highway. The Council agreed that '*application be made to The Local Government Board to issue an Order putting in force the provisions of Section 19 of the Private Street Works Act 1892 in this Rural District with respect to Ashleigh Road, Solihull and investing the Council with all the powers rights duties capabilities liabilities and obligations which an Urban District Council may by the adoption of the said Act acquire under those provisions so far as regards the said street.*' The application was made on 24 April to The Local Government Board who responded on 24 May that they would issue such an order. This was done on 6 June and on 4 July 1905 Solihull Council agreed unanimously that Ashleigh Road be declared a highway repairable by the inhabitants at large.

Individual houses & pairs of semi-detached properties, on plots of varying widths but a common depth (80yds 1ft 6ins), were designed by different architects. Ernest H.Wigley (1869-1947) who worked from 121 Colmore Row, Birmingham, was described as an architect & surveyor in the 1901 Census and became an LRIBA[5] in 1911. He was the architect for Nos 1, 14, 16 & 18; almost certainly Nos 7 & 9, 11 & 13, 15 & 17, 19, 31 & 33; and

---

[5] *A Licentiate of the Royal Institute of British Architects was an architect who lacked basic educational qualifications but had demonstrated competence in the design of buildings.*

Warwickshire County Record Office Ref: PH 372/68

*Motor accident at the junction of Ashleigh Road and Warwick Road in 1914. Note the curve of the wall of No 1 on the right. It was for cars like these that the early coach houses had given way to motor houses.*

possibly No12. He lived at No 17 from 1906 until 1925. Hipkiss & Stephens of Birmingham designed No 10. Samuel Cooper Stephens (1875-1915) was articled to Dunn & Hipkiss of Birmingham before going to Berlin for a short time as assistant to Ernst Ebelhard von Ihne. He established an independent practice with F.W.Hipkiss in Birmingham between 1901-09, and was made an LRIBA in 1911.[6] Ewen Harper (1853-1920) designed No 21. He attended the Birmingham School of Art in 1865 and then worked as a science and art master in South Kensington, before being articled to David Smith & Son. He started in independent practice in 1876 with his brother J.Alfred Harper from 1897. An FRIBA in 1907, his practice was in Corporation Street, Birmingham by 1911.[7] He lived in a house in Silhill Hall Road, which he designed. De Lacy-Aherne of 5 Waterloo Street, Birmingham designed No 20. All these were built between 1905 & 1913. The Ordnance survey of 1913 (published in 1917) showed that 34 plots had been developed, and that the trees along the pavements had been planted.

After World War I Satchwell & Roberts of Birmingham designed No 32 (a bungalow) in 1919 and maybe No 36. Williams & Boddy of Acocks Green designed No 34. John Burgess Surman (1885-1958) designed No 37. Born in Edgbaston and educated at Bromsgrove School, he was articled to E.Whitwell & Son in Birmingham and studied at the city's School of Art. He was a lecturer there from 1912-26 and Deputy Director for six years. He then set up in private

[6] *Information from Mrs Ruth Mosley of the Birmingham & Five Counties Architectural Association Trust.*
[7] *Ibid.*

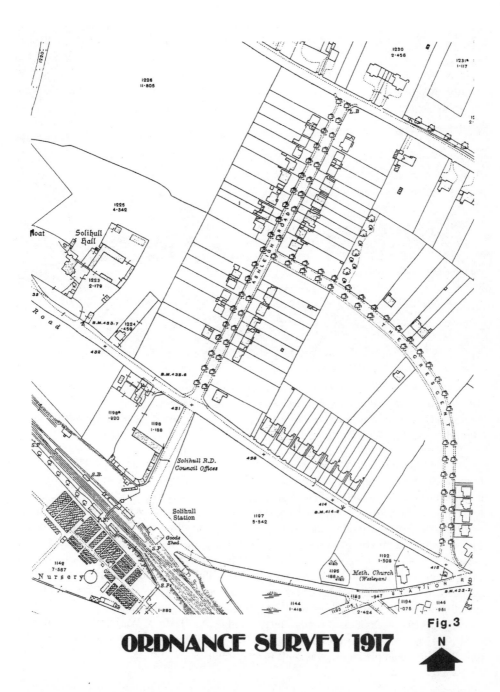

# ORDNANCE SURVEY 1917

Fig.3

N

*Plan of the Ashleigh Road area in 1917 from the Ordnance Survey 1:2500 map.*

*Postcard of Ashleigh Road from the south about 1930, showing the junction with Streetsbrook Road. Note the absence of road markings, the fence of No 38 and the old street sign. The limes have grown. The bungalow at No 32 can be seen as the fourth building on the left. No 37, designed by J.B.Surman, is second on the right.*

practice in partnership with W.T Benslyn, later G.Scott Kelly and his son, J.L.T. Surman.[8] Peter Hing (1885-1961) designed No 38 in 1922 and 28a in 1954. Aged 21 he had joined Wigley as an apprentice in 1906, and had then worked for Norman Shaw in London for several years.[9] He returned to Birmingham and practised from 121 Colmore Row, Wigley's former offices.

One other house, No 37a, dates from 1967. The bungalow (No 32) was demolished in 1996 and replaced by a house completed in 2000. There are thus 38 houses dating from 1904 to the 1920s, plus 3 from after World War II. Three other houses (532 Warwick Road built in 1929, 39 The Crescent built in 1936, & 112 Silhill Hall Road built in 1971) have boundaries on to Ashleigh Road, and thus were included within the Conservation Area created in November 1985 although they are not covered in this book.

The builders of the houses remain largely unknown. Baker & Warr of Camp Hill built No 4; Bragg of Solihull No 10; and Charles J.Grove of Dorridge No 37. Construction times were short, for example No 37 was built in six months.

---

[8] *Information from Mrs Ruth Mosley of the Birmingham & Five Counties Architectural Association Trust.*
[9] *Ibid.*

## CHANGES OVER THE YEARS

All the original houses had a number of similar features characteristic of the Edwardian period such as roof pitch, gables, casement windows, porches and timbered decoration, although differing in details. The regular building line, set 10 yards behind the front boundary walls of newly cut sandstone with a battlemented top, together with the wooden gates, gives a deceptively uniform and dull appearance to the road on early postcards, when the regularly planted lime trees were still only saplings. Over the years the streetscape has matured and softened. The avenue of limes has grown and houses and gardens have become more individual. In addition to necessary repairs and replacements, alterations have been made in response to developments in society and technology and to the different requirements and tastes of the occupants.

### Streetscape

The garden walls have become weathered, the stones rounded and lichen covered. Some of the original five courses have been reduced, removed or replaced by incongruous brick or artificial stone. No 38 never had a sandstone wall; its wooden fence has been replaced. The gates, once necessary to keep out cattle wandering from the fields behind Solihull Hall and nearer the village, have gone, although some sturdy gateposts remain (No 25). Entrances have been widened and drives enlarged to accommodate larger vehicles and two- or three-car families. Many drives, once of ash or gravel like the pavements, were later covered with tarmac; more recently the trend has favoured brick (Nos 24 & 26). Front gardens are now divided by a mixture of hedges and shrubbery, rhododendrons and holly doing particularly well, but there are occasional walls using stones from the front (No 6), and traces of the original low iron fences (between Nos 14 and 16).

At the road side, some of the original avenue of limes have been removed, leaving gaps. They are reaching the end of their natural life. All have been trimmed of their lower branches to increase visibility for increasing traffic, including busses and lorries.

The first street lamps were cast iron and probably gas-lit; the present 'plain suburban columns' look out of place. The conservation booklet said that lanterns on steel columns would be more ornamental and enhance the street lighting, but no move has been made to introduce them. Sadly the old street signs were damaged and replaced by modern, simpler designs. The red telephone box, just in Warwick Road, was lost about 1985 when BT installed a modern kiosk. There is still an original Edward VII post-box outside No 1a, one of the two remaining in Solihull, although with an ugly modern attachment to take part of the postman's load.

27 of the original 38 houses were built with 'coach' and later 'motor' houses with pitched roofs, containing lofts accessed by vertical wooden ladders. These were linked into the design and sometimes joined to the garage next door (17/19). Later garages were built beside No 9 and 11 in 1948 and Nos 13 and 15 in 1956. The semi-detached pair, Nos 16 and 18, which are at a slightly higher level than the street and without space at the side, were given planning permission that year to convert existing cellars into garages, with a steep slope up to street level. Some garages were later extended to accommodate the later, longer cars (No 14) and had double doors to the blue brick floored yard at the back. Here washing would be hung, well out of sight of the neighbours, and tradesmen would come through to

# ASHLEIGH ROAD CONSERVATION AREA

**Key**

— **Boundary of Conservation Area**       **Important hedges**

● **Important Trees**

*Plan of the Ashleigh Road Conservation Area designated in 1985, with a key to house numbers.*

the side door where there was a bell. Only the postman would go to the front door, using the small, ornate, cast-iron letter box, adequate in the early days for the smaller sized envelopes and postcards, but now inadequate and awkward for the size and quantity of mail received by the normal household, although several remain in use. Adjacent to the yard were further outhouses with a pitched roof including an outside toilet (for domestic staff and gardeners) and stores for coal, logs and garden tools.

**The Second World War**
When war broke out in September 1939 there was great activity. Air raid shelters were hastily built or excavated. In the *Warwickshire County News* for 16 September 1939 the *Man of Warwick* reported, *Solihull shelter at Ashleigh Road corner now finished. Heavily sandbagged it bears scrawled inscription over entrance support – 'the better 'ole'*. Along the Warwick Road there were notices advertising nearby air raid shelters and the number they could hold. One in Olton advertised 90 spaces. In Ashleigh Road several houses had shelters built, or made use of their cellars. No 7 had a trap door made into their living room from the cellar as an additional escape route. No 25 has its shelter under the front lawn, reached from the cellar, and No 37 has an Anderson shelter at the end of its garden. The nearest bombs that fell were in Poplar Road in 1940, and in Alston Road in 1944 when several people were killed. The explosions would have been felt by Ashleigh Road residents who would also be used to seeing the searchlights based at Ravenshaw, and hearing the anti aircraft guns in Damson Lane and Lode Lane.

Blackout regulations were severe. Newspapers record people prosecuted for infringements but also accidents which occurred to pedestrians, cyclists and motor cyclists who could not see where they were going or be seen. They were told to wear something white. Gas masks were advised and, if one had to go out during a raid, one reader in 1939 suggested wearing a colander on one's head, (in those days they were made of metal.) Facing the end of Ashleigh Road in Warwick Road was the Food Office where ration cards were obtained and shopkeepers had to return the coupons used every week. At the other end was the Fire Station in Streetsbrook Road, with the air-raid siren on its roof; its engines were on duty in Coventry when it was so badly bombed in November 1944. Older Solihull residents still remember seeing the red glow in the sky as it burned.

**Front Elevations**
Since the Second World War several houses have been extended, usually without spoiling the proportions or appearance of the houses, although sometimes the symmetry of pairs has been affected. Nos 22 and 27 built additional rooms over the garage, No 8 added a small room over the front door. At No 1, Abbeyfield, additional accommodation has been made using the garage and it now has a bridge to 1A which allows one housekeeper to monitor both properties when necessary. In No 12 in about 1987 the insertion of sky-lights allowed the creation of extra bedrooms on the second floor. No 21 had a covered stairway with a separate entrance built on the north side at the time it was made into flats. At the front of houses porches have been filled in a variety of ways and even completely remodelled (No 6). Some chimneys have been capped or removed and roofs retiled (No 14 in 1995.) Efforts have been made to use matching materials and to copy the distinctive ridge and

corner tiles. While most of the houses with timbering are painted black and white, considered 'traditional', the original colours were often blue and white or brown and cream.

Some houses have a plain or flat garden elevation. With others the architect has made the back as attractive as the front. No 14 had a porch, on the plan called a verandah, between the kitchen and then dining room, and a little later a crazy-paving terrace was made with a step down to the lawn. Nos 23 and 25 shared an open verandah which was later glazed and later still removed altogether. In the 1990s, some garden terraces became patios and then were built over and extended as conservatories, carefully designed, were added to kitchen and living areas, for example at Nos 20 and 21.

**Internal Changes**
A separate study could be made of internal changes to the original houses and the features introduced in the later ones. Early houses would have had a gas-fired geyser in the bathroom and open or perhaps gas fires in bedrooms, as well as the main fireplaces in the living and dining rooms. The effect of the introduction and improving technology of central heating and plumbing systems must have been great. Some of the Art Deco stained glass used inside as well as in external windows has been repaired, removed or replaced. Certain houses had plaster moulded ceilings put into the main rooms in the 1920's by Maples who sent craftsmen up from London.

Rooms have been thrown together and redivided according to the demands of the family. As most houses originally had servants the kitchen, scullery and larder were well separated from the living and dining rooms and usually only had a view of the yard or, over a high windowsill, of the street, but not of the garden to preserve the family's privacy. Post Second World War conditions changed. Windows and even doors were made to the garden from the kitchen to make a large family kitchen/dining and living area. The original owners would not recognise many of the kitchens of today. Gone are most of the white stone sinks, the wooden draining boards, the zinc wash-boilers, the kitchen range, the scrubbed wooden tables, the open wooden shelves and aluminium saucepans and quarry tiled floors. Now in the fully modernised kitchen all is stainless steel and pine or formica, fitted cupboards, split level cookers, dishwashers, microwaves and the latest modern gadgets. The freezer and washing machine are probably in the utility room, one of the original outhouses.

The original houses of Ashleigh Road were family homes well built to attractive designs which have remained in vogue. But, at the same time, they have been capable of adaptation to needs and fashions of each period. Provided they continue to be well maintained they should be good for another 100 years.

## SOCIAL & ECONOMIC ANALYSIS

It is interesting to analyse the social and economic background of Ashleigh Road over four periods - prior to World War I; between the wars; after World War II up to 1965; and a final twenty year timeslot 1965-1985. The number of houses increased from 34 in the first period to 41 by the final period, but the quality of the data varies depending on how many owners each house had during each of the periods and also on the amount of information that it has been possible to obtain.

**Occupations**

The number of professionals amongst the, mainly male, heads of household grew over the four periods. An accountant, lawyer and architect were amongst the six professionals before WWI and, besides increasing their representation, they were joined by the first doctor, banker and a retired army major in the second period. Ministers of religion arrived with the conversion of No 23 into the Methodist Manse in 1958 and the Anglican Chaplain to Solihull School in 1963. Teachers were represented from 1968.

Manufacturers were a significant proportion of the breadwinners up until WWII. Silverplate, electroplate, steel pin, steel toy, lamp and nuts/bolts were amongst the artefacts their companies made, and there were several manufacturing jewellers. Hugh ALDIS of the famous optical instrument makers lived at No 16 from 1919-1938. Since 1945 a number of company directors have lived in Ashleigh Road, but not necessarily of manufacturing companies. Craftsmen were a feature of the first two periods especially up to 1914, eg letter cutter, silversmith, bookbinder, tinsmith and tailor, but disappeared completely thereafter.

There was a coal merchant and a few commercial managers, eg of a cycle works, and a printer's traveller, before WWI. These grew after 1918 with the arrival of other merchants (fruit, wine/spirit, timber), an antique dealer and a motor engineer. A political agent is difficult to categorise but has been placed amongst these managers, as have company executives and local government officers. The latter were represented by Albert STAINTON (Collector of Poor Rates) of No 29 from 1908, but their number - like those who work in service industries - have grown over the years.

In each period there have been several widows/spinsters living in the road, the former normally arriving when already widowed. A number, however, have stayed in a house after their husband had died.

A statistical summary of the above is as follows:

| Period | Professional | Manufacturers | Craftsman & Com'l Managers | Merchants | Widows Known | Total |
|---|---|---|---|---|---|---|
| Before WWI | 5 | 9 | 7 | 4 | 2 | 27 |
| 1918-1939 | 13 | 20 | 5 | 17 | 6 | 61 |
| 1945-1964 | 20 | 10 | 1 | 9 | 6 | 46 |
| 1965-1984 | 17 | 4 | Nil | 7 | 3 | 31 |

An interesting feature is the number of servants. In the period between the wars 24 houses (62%) had one - and in some instances two - living-in servants, invariably female. No comparison can be made with the pre-WW I period since at that time females were not listed on the electoral roll. In the period 1945-1964 it is difficult to distinguish between servants, lodgers and companions: six houses appear to still have had a servant, at least until the mid-1950s, and 10 (including those houses that had been divided into two parts) had lodgers.

**Mortgages / Rentals**

Prior to WWI, when there were 34 houses, at least 10 (and possibly 4 others) were rented by the occupants (unfortunately no rental figures were quoted). Three had mortgages on them (with private investors, not building socities or banks): the interest rates were 4%.

In the second period, when there were 39 houses, only Nos 15 & 17 were rented (until 1925), but at least six were mortgaged (half with building societies/banks) with interest rates of 5% -6%. In the two periods after WWII a few houses (eg Nos 12, 20, 28) were leased for varying periods, generally because their owners worked abroad: this continues today in at least one instance. It would appear that at any one time well over half the properties were mortgaged. Interest rates varied widely from 3.5% to 14.5%.

**House Prices**

Sixteen current owners have allowed me access to the deeds of their house, and this enables the rise in house prices to be examined. In any one period prices naturally varied with the differing size of the houses and, since the 1960s, gardens. The rear of No 21 was sold for separate development in 1962; No 20 in 1964; and No 39 in 1965. The condition of the property, how quickly the owner/executors wished to sell, and the number of potential buyers were also important factors.

Up until 1914 individual properties usually changed hands at around £1,000, although No 4 was bought for only £700 in 1912. This was only £100 over the minimum price specified in the restrictive covenant made when the land was sold in 1903. Between 1916-21 prices had risen to the range £1,100 to £2,000, although No 19 exceeded this in 1920 with the astronomical price of £3,100 - the highest price that would be obtained for any property in Ashleigh Road until after World War II. For the rest of the 1920s & 1930s prices declined. Mrs Billingham, now widowed, received only £1,800 for No 19 in 1926. No 14, bought for £2,600 in 1922, sold for only £1,750 in 1936; and No 39 went from £2,620 in 1926 to only £1,800 in 1940. Generally the price drop was 10% to 15%.

By the late 1940s/early 1950s the price range for houses in Ashleigh Road was between £3,250 (Nos 11 & 13) and £6,000 (Nos 10 & 14). The minimum in the 1960s was £4,500 (No 2), whilst the first houses to achieve five figures were No 39 (£12, 250 in 1964, albeit from a developer) & No 20 (£10,250 in 1966 despite loss of land). As elsewhere, prices rose sharply in the 1970s so that £30,000 was common in the middle of that decade and substantially more by the end. The early 1980s saw prices around £70,000 when, besides inflation, a further boost was the creation of the Conservation Area in 1985. By 1990 six figure sums had been reached, and after 2000 £0.5 million was required for the larger properties.

On 4 June 1976 The Money Programme on BBC2 television devoted part of its half hour to Ashleigh Road. Produced by Andrew Clayton, it tried to demonstrate the wealth of the residents, but only a few of those invited were willing to take part.

**Continuity**

There has been a greater continuity of residents in Ashleigh Road than is perhaps usual elsewhere. Families have retained properties over several generations with individuals remaining in residence for many years; couples have moved from one house to another within the Road; and young people living in the Road have married each other.

No 33 has never been on the market since it was built. The first occupant (before 1910) was Mrs DEAKIN, who bequeathed it to her daughter Ada DEWBURY. The latter's son Bill, born in the house in 1921, still lives there. The LANCASTERs occupied No 25 from 1909-96, with Bessie living in the house for 56 years. Other families with long ownerships have been the PETRIEs at No 21 (1908-73), the DUNNs at No 36 (1934-84), and the SMITHs at No 13 (1907-55). Two other individuals have lived for 51 years in the same house: Albert SHEPPARD at No 34 (1921-72) and Ruth PATTERSON at No 35 (1931-82).

Residents have liked Ashleigh Road so much that several have moved within its length. William & Elizabeth CHAMBERLAIN lived at No 15 (1907-12) & No 4 (1912- 30); John & Caroline PARTRIDGE at No 11 (1906-16) & No 20 (1916-21); Henry & Adora WOOD at No 3 (1921-23) & No 36 (1923-28); Kate MORAN at No 32 (1924-46) & No 6 (1946-54); and Malcolm & Janet GARDNER at No 31 (1974-80) & No 12 (1980-86). Mrs ZAIR lived at No 16 with her husband from 1907-16 and then, after his death, at No 3 from 1923-54. Herbert & Mary PERIAM were at No 10 (1910-13) & No 15 (1920-23). Samuel & Ann FOSTER lived at No 2 from 1919-47, and their son & his wife at No 7 from 1934-52. John ROWLANDS was at No 35 between 1908-27 and his sister Winifred CHATTERLEY at No 7 from 1907-15. Peter FOX was at No 26 from 1962-68 and his sister Pam JOHNSON has lived since 1961 at No 2.

There are two instances of young people living in the road marrying each other. Cecil CONSTANTINE of No 11 married Edith TUSTAIN of No 12 in 1931; and Raymond SHEPPARD of No 34 married Florence LANCASTER of No 25 in 1933.

Although none of the residents over the years has lived to be a centenarian, several have survived to a great age. Dorothy CHALLENS of No 30 was 98 when she died in 1989; Bessie LANCASTER of No 25 was 93 when she died in 1995; Mary Ann COLLINS (No 26) was 91 on her death in 1927; and Foster GOULD (No 17) was also 91 when he died in 1964. Albert SHEPPARD was 93 when he left No 34 for a nursing home where he died 18 months later in 1974. Eliza HEELEY (No 28) was 92 when she died in a nursing home in 1937.

A final example of continuity is the telephone number of certain houses. No 10 has had the number 0108 since 1928, and No 33 has been 0818 since 1932.

## Conclusion

Ashleigh Road was developed as a well-to-do Edwardian residential street, and so it has remained. Whilst, on the evidence of the Will Index, a few of its occupants have been wealthy, most appear over the years to have had average middle class incomes. Several residents have achieved distinction in their business, profession or the community, and a few have been awarded honours. The history of the road is a microcosm of a particular social environment extending over a century.

# 4. HOUSES 1 TO 21

## No 1    ESTCOURT / ABBEYFIELD

The house was designed in 1907 by Ernest H.Wigley, architect & surveyor of 121 Colmore Row, Birmingham, and resident at No 17 Ashleigh Road, for Charles Rowe LANDER, a Birmingham jeweller, whose business premises were at 70 Great Hampton Street, Birmingham. Its format includes red bricks and tiles, applied timber framing, casement windows and a 6 sided bay window, which only occurs here and at No 30; elsewhere in the road the 5 sided bay window is more common. The original plans exist. They show a full and generous range of domestic accommodation. The front door opened into a 'Sitting Hall' with the side door opening into a 'Staircase Hall'. The kitchen was served by a Larder, Pantry, Scullery and 'China Pantry'. China Pantries were a common feature of the earlier Ashleigh Road houses. On the first floor were four bedrooms for the family and on the second (attic) floor there were a further three rooms, presumably for domestic staff. The garage was described as a 'Motor House' though it owed its form to a coach house, and there was a loft above for fodder & tackle. Ernest Wigley had appendicitis during the construction of the house, and his responsibilities were taken over by his colleague, Frederick Wigley, who was no relation[1].

Charles Lander had been recorded in the 1881 Census as an apprentice aged 16. He was the third of five sons of Tertins Lander, aged 55, a merchant, who lived with his wife Susan aged 47 (born in Kandy, Ceylon) at 69 Soho Hill, Handsworth. Charles had left home by 1891 but his father, now widowed, still lived at the same address with two sons and a daughter, a housekeeper and a domestic servant. Charles married Emma Ann Phillips on 17 April 1890 at Wretham Road Church, Handsworth. Aged 24, she was the daughter of William Phillips, a stamper of Great Hampton Street, Birmingham[2]. They lived at *Estcourt* until about 1926, but never installed a telephone. They moved to 67 Dovehouse Lane, which they also called *Estcourt*. Emma died of cancer[3] on 12 May 1947 and Charles on 1 November 1953. Probate for their estates, £974-15-6d & £38,907-0-7d respectively, was granted to their son.

Charles & Emma had a son (Charles) Herbert and a daughter Muriel. Herbert, born on 29 July 1893, married Dorothy Mary Throckmorton (b 28 April 1896) of Coughton Court. They lived at 85 St Bernards Road. In old age he was lame and could not get upstairs to see his invalid wife. He died on 6 November 1984 (worth £118,171) and his wife a few days later[4]. At their joint funeral at Olton Monastery the priest said that *'in life they were separated by a staircase, but now they are together in heaven'*[5]. They had a daughter Mary P. who, unmarried, continues to live at 85 St Bernards Road, and twins, names unknown.

---

[1] *Information from Mrs M.Hutton, who was Frederick's daughter. Frederick was the brother of William Edward Wigley (1880-1942), the oil and watercolour painter.*
[2] *Marriage Certificate*
[3] *Information from Miss Molly Bullock*
[4] *GRO Index for 1984 [Solihull S. 1184 34 0053]*
[5] *Information from Miss Molly Bullock*

*Nos 1a and 1, the Abbeyfield houses, in 2002.*

Charles and Emma's daughter Muriel, born in 1902[6], attended Malvern Hall School and married Leslie Nock, whose father was a Governor of the school. They lived in Dovehouse Lane, which was why her parents moved there from Ashleigh Road. During a Second World War air raid, the latter walked across the road to the Nocks' air raid shelter, she wearing a tea cosy surmounted by a colander and he with a raised umbrella[7].

The next occupant of No 1 was Dr Donald Carmichael THOMAS[8] who was one of Dr Quinet's partners[9]. Although he never had a surgery at his house, Dr Thomas installed a telephone before 1930, Solihull 155 which became 0155 in 1931. He had married Norah Alice Couldrey in 1916[10], and their son Oliver Somerville was born in 1918[11]. They had a servant - Elsie Windsor was there in 1929/30, although she had left by 1931, and Helen White in 1934/35[12].

---

[6] *GRO Index for Q/E June 1902 [West Bromwich 6b 876]*

[7] *Information from Miss Molly Bullock*

[8] *Electoral Roll 1927*

[9] *Information from Miss Kathleen Saunders. Dr Quinet was the well known Belgian born doctor who practised from The Doctor's House, now called Quinet House, on the corner of Warwick Road and Lode Lane*

[10] *GRO Index for Q/E March 1916 [Paddington 1a 111]*

[11] *GRO Index for Q/E March 1918 [Hampstead 1a 732]*

[12] *Electoral Rolls*

*Newspaper picture of Douglas Fairbanks jnr and Gertrude Lawrence with Dr. Bernays at a RSPCA Garden Party in the garden of No 1 in 1934.*

On Wednesday 13 June 1934 a great occasion took place in the garden. *The Warwick County News* had a full report on the following Saturday under the headline 'FILM STARS IN SOLIHULL'. *Two famous filmstars – Miss Gertrude Lawrence and Mr Douglas Fairbanks, jun – came to Solihull on Wednesday to open a garden fete at 'Estcourt', Ashleigh Road (the residence of Dr and Mrs Carmichael Thomas) in aid of the Solihull Auxiliary of the Royal Society for the Prevention of Cruelty to Animals. There was a large attendance, the majority ladies, and quite a crowd assembled outside the gates to catch a glimpse of the noted visitors.*

*Dr A.V.Bernays, who presided at the opening ceremony, spoke of the enormous amount the public owed to the dramatic profession for lifting them out of the drabness of ordinary life. It was remarkably true that if one wanted a thing done, busy people were more likely to do it than people with unlimited leisure. There were two views quite commonly held with regard to the RSPCA, said Dr Bernays. One was that the Society was rolling in money and the other was that there was no cruelty to animals. Both were untrue. Birmingham had always been rather a drag on the Society which had responded to the City's claims in a most generous way. He hoped the result of this fete would be of great financial assistance to the Society.*

*Miss Lawrence expressed her pleasure at being able to support a cause so near to her heart. She herself was an owner and a great lover of animals. She said she appreciated the generosity of Dr & Mrs Thomas in lending their beautiful house to make the fete possible. Miss Lawrence was presented with a bouquet and there was a charming scene as she impulsively plucked a flower from the rest and gave it to the little girl who had made the presentation. Mr Fairbanks professed himself to be 'oratorically impotent', but nevertheless he made a neat little speech, which kept his audience constantly amused. He closed with the rather ingenuous smile which is familiar to film-goers the world over.*

*A vote of thanks was accorded Miss Lawrence and Mr Fairbanks on the proposition of Mr Cope Gem, seconded by Mr B.W.Handley, and Dr & Mrs Thomas were thanked on the proposition of the Rev'd J.C.Adams.*

The two stars were appearing at the Birmingham Theatre Royal in *'The Winding Journey'*, which had begun its run the previous Monday. The newspaper also carried a picture of the fete, and another article headlined 'FILM STAR LIONISED'. *Every member of the fair sex, nowadays, between the ages of ten and seventy, has her favourite film star, and Douglas Fairbanks, jnr, seems to have his share of fair admirers in Solihull at any rate. There must have been 200 ladies at the fete at 'Estcourt', Dr & Mrs Thomas's beautiful home, on Wednesday, when 'Doug' performed the opening ceremony with Miss Gertrude Lawrence, and he must have given most of them his autograph.*

*Film folk are notoriously temperamental, but these famous stars are remarkably tractable, and posed for innumerable photographs (press and ordinary box cameras). They joined in the amusements too, and really seemed to be enjoying themselves. Being a film star, one supposes, is not all beer and skittles, and this fete will probably stand out in their minds as a very happy and 'homely' affair.*

Douglas Fairbanks jnr's association with Solihull continued. During and after the War he was president of the Cooperative for American Remittances in Europe (CARE), which sent food parcels to the needy. At a ceremony at the Commonwealth Gift Centre in London in July 1949 he was personally thanked by Councillor Maurice Walker, chairman of Solihull Council. Only that week *'one of Solihull's grand old men had received a monster box of goodies sent by the kindly folk of America to their less fortunate cousins over here – a gesture of friendship that means so much to Britain in these grim days'.*

The house was empty in 1940[13]. (Joseph) Leslie & Adeline Patti (nee Purden, known as Pat) SHEPERDSON were in residence by 1945, with their sons (Joseph) Peter born in 1927[14] and David born in 1930[15], both of whom went to Solihull School. David died from tuberculosis aged 10 in 1940[16]. On 21 July 1943[17] the Sheperdsons adopted 2 daughters (twins), Valerie Mary & Veronica Ann, both of whom became nurses[18]. Leslie Shepherdson had originally worked for the Bank of England in Birmingham but as a young man, around 1930, had contacted tuberculosis. He was medically retired by The Bank with a pension of £50 pa (fixed) as he was not expected to live. In fact he made a complete recovery and became the managing director of a paint company[19].

During the war Leslie, known as Shep, was the Air Raid Precaution Warden for Ashleigh Road, and he had a tent on the pavement outside his house. In it was kept a large

---

[13] *Kelly's Directory for Warwickshire 1940*

[14] *GRO Index for Q/E December 1927 [Solihull 6d 1133]*

[15] *GRO Index for Q/E June 1930 [Solihull 6d 1296]*

[16] *GRO Index for Q/E September 1940 [Birmingham 6d 563]*

[17] *Adoption [Volume 186, Entries 92654 & 5]*

[18] *Information from Mrs Muriel Waters (nee Bragg)*

[19] *Information from Mr George Pemberton*

handbell for sounding a warning. One day a small boy stole the bell, but was ordered by his father to take it back to Shep. Grateful to have it returned, Shep promised the boy could have it after the war ended – and five years later kept his promise[20].

Shep was a local councillor and served as Mayor in 1962/63. In that capacity he hosted The Queen's visit to the Borough on 25 May 1962 when she formally opened the new Civic Hall. This was the first visit of a reigning Sovereign to Solihull[21]. Shep was also a Magistrate and a County Councillor. He worked tirelessly for local charities and did much for Sunnymount, the home for the disabled in Knowle. Shepherdson Court in Rayner House was named after him. Shep was a Governor of several schools including St Martins and Tudor Grange Grammar School for Boys. He also ran a youth club at Olton Chapel Hall called The Good Companions. Pam Johnson nee Fox (now at No 2) was a member. She also played tennis on the grass court which the Shepherdsons (who were very keen on the game) had on the north side of their house where their garden extended to the Warwick Road. Mrs SHEPHERDSON was keen on cricket and frequently travelled to Edgbaston to watch matches[22] In 1950 Walter & Dorothy Saunders were living with them, but had disappeared by 1955[23]. The Shepherdson's telephone number was Solihull 1512. When they left, they went to live at 5 Parklands on Blossomfield Road. They both died in 1988: Shep aged 86 at home on 22 March worth under £70,000; and Pat aged 87 at Green Gables, 54 Sandbach Road, Congleton on 26 November worth £116,953.

The occupants in 1960 were John & Gladys WILKINSON. The telephone number was changed to Solihull 5331. John Wilkinson was a chartered mechanical engineer. They were the last family before the house became an Abbeyfield.

In 1961 the Rector of Solihull, Canon Hartley, held a 'parish life conference' led by a hard hitting Australian priest named Bruce Reed. The latter convinced the conference that their own brand of Christianity was too parochial and that they should look outwards to the needs of the community. From this The Abbeyfield, Solihull, Society was born. The Society raised £1200 which, together with a small loan from St Alphege Parochial Church Council and a mortgage, enabled it to buy No 1 Ashleigh Road for an Abbeyfield Home which opened in 1963[24]. The house was altered and then extended in 1976.

Following a recommendation of its Housing Committee early in 1973, Solihull Council approved '*a scheme to build a two-storey house to accommodate eight old people and a housekeeper in the grounds. The Finance Committee was urged to consider giving the Society a loan with interest.*' This formed a separate Abbeyfield, known as 1a Ashleigh Road. On 21 May 1991 Prince Charles, as Patron of the Abbeyfield Society, came to Ashleigh Road (which was completely sealed off for the afternoon) to reopen No 1 following a major refurbishment: a plaque in the inner hall proudly commemorates this event. There were further alterations in 1996, when a lift was installed, and in 2001 when

---

[20] *Information from Mrs Nesta Hurst*
[21] *Slightly over 40 years after this event, on 2 July 2002, The Queen opened the Touchwood Shopping Centre which was partially built on the site of the Civic Hall, demolished in 1998.*
[22] *Information from Mrs Diana Mitchell MBE*
[23] *Electoral Roll 1955*
[24] *St Alphege Parish Magazine March 2001*

*Nos 3 and 5 in 2002, a handed pair with semi-detached garages, designed by E.H.Wigley.*

a passageway was constructed joining the first floor of No 1 to the top floor of No 1a to allow more economical night staffing[25].

### No 3    BETHERLIE / COLINTON / LISMOYNE / WILLINGDON

Nos 3 & 5 are a handed pair of detached houses with semi-detached garages, the valley between the latter's roofs acting as a line of symmetry. They were obviously designed by the same architect, but the original drawings no longer exist. They share some of E.H.Wigley's characteristics found at No 1 and his other documented houses in the road (Nos 14, 16 & 18), but it cannot be proved that he designed these. Their frontage is distinguished by a five sided two storey bay window, and the garages share applied timber detail similar to the houses. They are virtually contemporary (ie 1907/8) with, although smaller than, No 1[26]. No 3 has a frontage of 16yds 1ft 6ins and the standard depth of 80yds 1ft 6ins.

Joseph Wells, the developer, retained the freehold. This house may initially have been known as *Littlemore*, and, if so, his first tenant was Joshua Edward CARTWRIGHT, who was listed in 1908[27]. Mrs CRIPWELL was certainly the tenant in 1912[28] and she named the house *'Betherlie'*. Her husband was Albert Cripwell[29]. He had been recorded as a scholar

---

[25] *Information from Mrs Sue Hewitt*
[26] *Ashleigh Road Conservation Area by Simon Herrick*
[27] *Kelly's Directory for Warwickshire 1908*
[28] *Kelly's Directory for Warwickshire 1912*
[29] *Electoral Roll 1912*

aged 9 in the 1881 Census, living at home in Sycamore Road, Harborne (then in Staffordshire). Albert was the third of eleven children, and eldest of six sons, of James Cripwell (aged 39), a commercial clerk, & Harriett (30), his wife. In the 1901 Census he was shown as an Incorporated Accountant, aged 29, still living at home which was now 46 South Road, Smethwick. He married Kate Cooper on 29 April 1909 at the Old Church, Smethwick. Aged 24, she was the daughter of the late Tom Cooper[30]. By the time they lived in Ashleigh Road, Albert had an office at 12 Cherry Street, Birmingham[31].

On 16 April 1913 Mr Wells mortgaged the property for £395 to A.W.Woolley (electroplater) of Kings Norton, H.F.Woolley (gentleman) of Bournmouth & T.W.Robinson (solicitor) of Birmingham. The interest rate was 4%.

By 1916[32] the tenant was Walter Andrew HARRISON, who renamed the house *'Colinton'*. In the 1881 Census, aged 31, he had been shown living at 12 Oliver Road, Birmingham, with his wife Eliza (also 31), daughter Dora Lilian (3) and son Percival Walter (5 months). Walter was described as an Electroplate Manufacturer Master, employing 21 men, 1 woman & 4 boys. At the age of 70, Walter Harrison bought the freehold of *Colinton* on 8 May 1920 for £1750 from Mr Wells, and on 9 August that year mortgaged the property for £1000 to G.Smith (gentleman) & H.F.Keep (merchant) both of Edgbaston and A.H.Fairburn (solicitor) of Dudley. The interest rate was 6%. Two months later, on 16 October, Mr Harrison died. The value of his estate was £8,827-12-9d.

The trustees of his estate (his daughter Dora & son Percival, of *Tyrol*, Alderbrook Road) sold *Colinton* on 16 June 1921 for £2000 to Mrs Adora WOOD, the wife of Henry Wood, a tinsmith, of 13 Holly Road, Handsworth. The Woods had two sons, William born in 1893[33], and Leonard born in 1899[34], and possibly a daughter Emily, though she was too young to be included in the electoral rolls. After only two years Mrs Wood sold the house on 5 November 1923 for £1700 and moved with her family to No 36.

The purchaser was Mrs Edith Harcourt ZAIR, a widow, of *Lismoyne*, Lydford, Devon. Previously, between 1906-16, Mrs Zair had lived with her husband as the first tenants of No 16. Mrs Zair renamed *Colinton* as *Lismoyne*. She also, on 6 November that year, mortgaged the property for £1700 to herself & J.W.Braithwaite (bank manager) of *Compton*, Streetsbrook Road. The interest rate was 5%. It is interesting to note that on 6 June 1925 Mrs Zair paid £2-7-4d to the Ministry of Agriculture & Fisheries to redeem the tithe for her property's share of the original fields Nos 1519 & 1520 which Mr Wells, the developer, had bought from Richard Chattock in 1903. By 1928[35] Mrs Zair had installed the telephone: her number was Solihull 44, which became 0044 with the introduction of four figure numbers three years later.

Mrs Zair did not live alone. The 1929 Electoral Roll recorded Hester M.Percival also living at Lismoyne: she may have been a relative or companion since she was still with Mrs

---

[30] *Marriage Certificate*
[31] *Birmingham & District Telephone Directory 1911*
[32] *Kelly's Directory for Warwickshire 1916*
[33] *GRO Index for Q/E December 1893 [West Bromwich 6b 810]*
[34] *GRO Index for Q/E March 1899 [West Bromwich 6b 805]*
[35] *Kelly's Directory for Warwickshire 1928*

Zair in 1950. In 1955 she had been replaced by Esther Maud Percival. The 1929-1931 Electoral Rolls also record Alfred Harcourt Zair. This was Mrs Zair's son, who had been born in 1907[36]. He became a medical practitioner in Ludlow, and on 12 February 1947 Mr Braithwaite's share of the mortgage was transferred to him. Thomas G.S.Grey also lived in the house from 1946 to 1948.

Mrs Zair died aged 88 on 13 November 1954 at the Queen Elizabeth Hospital, Edgbaston. Her estate was valued at £11,443-1s. Her executors (Dr A.H.Zair & Jane Zair, his wife, of Ashford Court, Ludlow) sold Lismoyne on 8 March 1955 for £4,200 to Percival John KING, company director, of 279 Warwick Road, Olton. He mortgaged the property on the same day for £3,780 to Solihull Borough Council. The interest rate was 3.5%. His wife was called Ann Richardson.

Two years later, on 29 April 1957, the property was bought for £6100 by Dorothy JACOBS (nee Hill), the wife of Alfred Edward Jacobs, a chartered accountant, of 12 Mirfield Road, Solihull. They had married in 1932[37]. Dorothy mortgaged the property, on 10 September 1957, for £1500 to her father, Oliver Hill (a retired builders manager) who lived with them. The interest rate was 6%. He died on 23 July 1965 and his will showed that Mr & Mrs Jacobs, his executors, had two sons, John Anthony born in 1938[38] and Peter, both of whom went to Solihull School[39]. The Jacobs family lived at *Lismoyne* for 13 years. Their telephone number was Solihull 1575.

On 9 September 1970 the house was sold for £11,500 to Frank Brownrigg TAYLOR & Jean TAYLOR, his wife, of 47 Whitchurch Road, Chester. After less than three years they sold it on 12 April 1973 for £29,000 to Albert (but called Alan) Henry Louis HOOPER of 8 Bromley Lane, Chislehurst, Kent. The rateable value was shown as £151. The telephone number was 705 7356.

William Howard VINE, chartered accountant, & Joan Rhaidr (nee Kendall), his wife, bought the property on 30 September 1977. They changed the house name from *Lismoyne* to *Willingdon*, and the telephone number became 0591. Their children, Andrew (born 22 January 1969, who married Julie Gibbins at Temple Balsall in November 2000), Nicola Claire (born in 1971), and Sarah Elizabeth (born 14 June 1973) grew up there before leaving home. Bill & Joan moved to Balsall Common in 1999.

They sold the property, now without a name, to Andrew and Rosalind SPITTLE who kindly provided all the Conveyance & Mortgage Indenture information above. They continue to live in the house with their young daughters, Katherine (born in 1995) and Lucy (born in 1997).

## No 5    St BRIAVELS / WITHDENE

The handed version of, and built at the same time as, No 3. It is not known who the first occupant was, but it is possible that it was Walter Stuart BROWN who was listed in Kelly's Directory in 1908 and on the electoral rolls in 1909 & 1910 at a house called *Moniave*. On

---

[36] *GRO Index for Q/E June 1907 [Solihull 6d 640*

[37] *GRO Index for Q/E September 1932 [Birmingham S. 6d 243*

[38] *GRO Index for Q/E December 1938 [Birmingham 6d 814]*

[39] *Information from Mrs Muriel Waters (nee Bragg)*

24 June 1911 Joseph Wells sold the property, known as *St Briavels,* for £1100 to John Smedley Crooke of 37/8 High Street, Birmingham, pawnbroker & jeweller, and Hubert Rowlands of 41 Temple Row, Birmingham, solicitor, the trustees of the late William Henry Wood. *St Briavels* had a frontage of 16yds 1ft 6ins and an area of 1328 sq yds: the owner was responsible for the fences on both the NE & SW sides of the land. The trustees invested heavily in Ashleigh Road as, on the same day, they also bought Nos 2, 7 & 9, 11 & 13 from Mr Wells.

In 1912 Joseph SUCKLING lived in the house and he was one of only three people in the road to have a telephone at this date. The number was Solihull 65 which, with the introduction of four figure numbers, became 0065 in 1931. Joseph had been born in 1883[40], the son of William Suckling, whose company were silver plate manufacturers in Albion Street, Birmingham. Described as a manufacturer, Joseph married Doris Gertrude Edman on 30 June 1908 at St Augustine, Edgbaston. Aged 21, she was the daughter of George Alfred Edman of 25 Westfield Road, Edgbaston[41]. On 4 April 1919 the Sucklings bought the freehold of the house, in which they had lived for at least seven years, for £1,275. The actual purchaser was Gertrude, rather than Joseph, and her signature was witnessed by Alice Gertrude Edman, probably her mother, of *The Bungalow,* Copt Heath. The conveyance refers to the house as *Withdene, formerly St Briavels,* but the electoral roll omits any name until 1930. This was unique in Ashleigh Road, where all the remaining houses were known by their names; numbers were not used until 1932.

Between 1929 & 1931 the Sucklings had a servant called Ann Sarah Wood. They stayed at *Withdene* until 1933 as the electoral roll of October that year showed the house as empty. On 20 November Gertrude, described as the wife of Joseph Suckling of *The Bungalow,* Copt Heath, mortgaged *Withdene* for £1200 to St Philips Benefit Building Society No 1. The interest rate was 4.5%. The mortgage was repaid on 23 June 1934, two days before Gertrude sold the freehold. Joseph died on 29 August 1971 at 1222 Warwick Road, Copt Heath worth £41,251.

The purchaser, for £1,300 on 25 June 1934, was (Clarence) Owen MORLEY of *Trentavon,* Lode Lane, manufacturer. He had married Alice Mabel Shipway in 1930[42], and they had twins - Marcus & Marcia - born in the house in 1934[43]. When the family came to *Withdene* they had a servant, Gladys Joyce Stringer. She was replaced by Joan Irene Dobson[44], who in turn gave way to Phyllis Melhuish in 1939. The telephone number was Solihull 0752. Owen's father was the principal of a paint company in which Owen nominally worked, but he never seemed to do very much except draw his salary[45]. He had become a director of the company by the time he sold the house.

On 8 March 1944 Arthur BISHOP of 114 Ladbroke Road, Solihull, bought the property for £2,750. He and his wife Dorothy stayed for nearly 20 years. Described as an engineer,

---

[40] *GRO Index for Q/E March 1883 [Birmingham 6d 39]*
[41] *Marriage Certificate*
[42] *GRO Index for Q/E September 1930 [Birmingham S. 6d 918]*
[43] *GRO Index for Q/E September 1934 [Birmingham 6d 556]*
[44] *Electoral Roll 1937*
[45] *Information from Mr George Pemberton*

Arthur Claude Bishop had married Dorothy Mary Jones at Bournville Church on 23 February 1924. Aged 28, a year older than her husband, she was the daughter of William Jones, a carpenter, of 26 Sycamore Road, Bournville[46]. Their son John Michael appeared in the 1946-48 Electoral Rolls. He had been born on 16 October 1925 and educated at Solihull School & Birmingham University where he read medicine. After qualifying as a physician, he did his national service in the Royal Army Medical Corps between 1949-51. He married Hilary Wishart in 1952 and had a son and a daughter. After various posts in The Queen Elizabeth Hospital, Edgbaston, he was appointed lecturer in medicine at Birmingham University in 1956 and Professor of Medicine in 1966. He retired in 1985 and moved to Warwick[47]. The Bishops also had a daughter, Rosemary, born in 1930[48], who was a keen horse rider[49]. Their telephone number at No 5 was Solihull 0830, and this remained the number for the next occupants. Dorothy Bishop died aged 67 in 1963[50] and Arthur in 1966[51].

Arthur Bishop had sold the house for £7,000 on 10 January 1964 to Geoffrey Norman GIBBONS of 96 Soho Road, Handsworth. Two days later Mr Gibbons raised a mortgage of £4,350 on the property from the Bingley Building Society at an interest rate of 6%. Further small sums were added between 1964-1975 to the loan, from what had become the Bradford & Bingley Building Society on 1 July 1964. Geoffrey lived in the house with his mother Gladys and that entry in the electoral roll was repeated until 1974, after which there was no entry for Gladys. Geoffrey married Hazel M.Paddock (nee Roden) in 1974[52]. She came with the three children from her previous marriage - Nicola Jane (born 17 June 1952), David (born 1954) and John (born 1959) The first two appeared in the 1975 & 1976 electoral rolls, and John in 1978. The Gibbons moved later that year to 1153 Warwick Road, Solihull, taking their telephone number (0830) with them.

Geoffrey had been born on 17 December 1927 and educated at Moseley Grammar School & Birmingham University where he read law. His national service between 1948-50 was in The Royal Army Service Corps; he was posted to Egypt and reached the rank of Acting Captain. He became an assistant solicitor with F.W.Oakley in 1952 and a partner in 1954. The practice became Blewitt Oakley in 1962 with Geoffrey as a partner, and this in turn became became Rowleys & Blewitts in 1970. He became the senior partner in 1980, and was a deputy circuit judge, Midland & Oxford Circuit, 1976-83[53]. Geoffrey served on the Solihull District Council from 1969 to 1998, and was Mayor in 1974/75 and 1984/85. He played a leading role in the Solihull Festival each May up until its demise in 2000. Now retired and living near Kenilworth, he is also a fine organist (St Ambrose Edgbaston 1946-59, Henley Parish Church 1959-97) and helps out at a number of local churches, including the private chapel – St James, Great Packington – of the Earl of Aylesford.

[46] *Marriage Certificate*
[47] *Birmingham Year Book 1989*
[48] *GRO Index for Q/E June 1930 [Birmingham S 6d 218]*
[49] *Information from Mrs Diana Mitchell MBE*
[50] *GRO Index for Q/E June 1963 [Solihull 9c 909]*
[51] *GRO Index for Q/E September 1966 [Solihull 9c 842]*
[52] *GRO Index for Q/E September 1974 [Birmingham 32 0960]*
[53] *Birmingham Year Book 1998*

Michael & Philippa GATES of 93 Links Drive, Solihull bought the property on 12 May 1978. Their elder daughter Hillary became 18 on 11 January 1981, and their younger daughter, Gillian, on 30 November 1983. Mr & Mrs GATES kindly loaned the deeds of their house to provide some of the above information.

## No 7    BRANSCOMBE

*'Numbers 7 & 9 are a handsome pair of semi-detached which date from about 1905. The 5 sided bay window to the drawing room of each house has a dentil-mould cornice and the drawing room fireplace is served by what could be called an 'inglenook' window. Many of the ground floor windows are decorated with stained glass. At the first floor there is a railing over the porches to prevent unlawful access from one house to another. The second floor gables are decorated with timber boarding.'*[54]

The 1907 Electoral Roll showed only 10 residents in Ashleigh Road, of whom a mere three had so far chosen the names of their houses. Percy Newton CHATTERLEY of *'Branscombe'* was one of these. The others were A.V.Martindale of *Newstead* No 12 and E.H.Wigley of *Kilmorna* No 17. Somewhat confusingly, Mrs Taylor in 1908 named her house, almost opposite, as *Bransford* (now No 6). Mr Chatterley stayed until after 1912[55]. He had been recorded aged 7 in the 1881 Census as the youngest of six children of John Bishop Chatterley, aged 54, a japanner & electroplate manufacturer, & his wife Clara (49) of 259 Birchfield Road, Handsworth. Percy, who also became a manufacturer, married Winifred Rowlands (born in 1875) at St Alphege Church on 4 September 1900[56]. She was the daughter of Edward Rowlands, a well known Birmingham solicitor who lived in Homer Road, Solihull, and the sister of John Arthur Rowlands who, in 1908, came to live at *The Bungalow,* No 35.

At the 1901 Census Percy and Winifred lived at *Beechcroft,* Warwick Road, Yardley. They had a son called Eric in 1906[57]. They left *Branscombe* during the First World War. Percy, by then of 3 West Pathway, Harborne, died aged 45 on 1 March 1919 but, for reasons unknown, probate for his estate worth £949-18-6d was not granted to his son, an electrical engineer, until 1954[58]. Winifred died aged 70 in 1945[59]. She is now commemorated on her brother's stone in St Alphege Churchyard: he died in 1954.

By 1916[60] Miss Florence Elizabeth HAMMOND had taken up residence. She had been born in 1874[61] and was recorded in the 1881 Census with her parents at 14 Eldon Place, Bradford. She was the sixth of seven daughters, and her father - Ezra - was described as a 'common brewer'. Florence remained at Branscombe until after 1932. She never installed a telephone. In the 1930/31 electoral roll Sarah Annie Bailey & Gladys Helena Ward Lewis,

---

[54] *Ashleigh Road Conservation Area by Simon Herrick*
[55] *Kelly's Directory for Warwickshire 1912*
[56] *Marriage Certificate*
[57] *GRO Index for Q/E March 1906 [Solihull 6d 655]*
[58] *Probate Index of Wills*
[59] *GRO Index for Q/E December 1945 [Birmingham 6d 573]*
[60] *Kelly's Directory for Warwickshire 1916*
[61] *GRO Index for Q/E March 1874 [Bradford 9b 169]*

presumably servants, lived with her. Florence moved to 1 Nevill Place, Hove. She died aged 68 at Hove Hospital, Sackville Road on 29 December 1942. Probate for her estate worth £24,576-6-1d was granted to The Public Trustee.

In October 1933 Athelstan Wardhaugh BLACKWELL, with his wife Bessie and daughter Bessie Kathleen, lived in the house with their servant Mary James. They had a telephone, Solihull 0729. Athelstan Blackwell had been recorded, aged 1, in the 1881 Census at home in Withen Lane, Liscard, Wallasey. His father, George Grove Blackwell aged 39, who had been born at Stratford-on-Avon, was a manganese merchant. His Irish mother Jane, also 39, was described as a mineral broker, and her mother, Jane Thompson (77), lived with them. Athelstan had four elder brothers and three elder sisters; an Italian servant made up the household. Athelstan, who became a mineral merchant, married Bessie Wilson at St Mary, Grassendale (Liverpool) on 7 February 1906. She was the daughter of Thomas Wilson, gentleman, of *Daylesford*, Grassendale Park[62]. Their daughter Bessie was born in 1908[63].

By October 1934[64] Horace Samuel Sproston and Maud FOSTER had arrived. He was the eldest son of Samuel and Annie Elizabeth Sproston Foster who lived at No 2 from 1918 to 1947. Whilst still serving as a Lieutenant in the Army, Horace had married (Ethel) Maud Dunford on 15 June 1918 at Linslade (Beds); his father & two sisters were amongst the witnesses[65]. He followed his father into the family coal merchant business, and had a depot at Knowle[66]. He installed a telephone on his arrival: its number was Solihull 0978. Horace & Maud had three children: Barbara Dunford born in 1920[67] who served in the forces during World War II[68]; Samuel Errington (known as Sam) born in 1921[69]; and Patricia A. born in 1932[70]. They also had a servant, Dorothy Rose Young, from 1937 to at least 1939: she may have been replaced by Joan Salmon, who served with the forces during the war. At home, the Fosters had a removable panel made in the front room floor to enable escape (in the event of the stairway being blocked) from the cellar, so that it could be used as an air raid shelter. The family remained at No 7 until after 1950. Horace died on 6 September 1952 aged 60 worth £21,974-2s, and Maud on 1 August 1985 aged 89: they share a tombstone in St Alphege Churchyard. After Sam Foster inherited the family business he extended it by buying Blackwells, the coal merchants at Hampton-in-Arden[71].

The Fosters were succeeded in 1952[72] by Richard John & Joan Winifred LEES, who arrived from Surrey. Their children, John and Patricia, appeared on the 1965 and 1967 electoral rolls respectively. Both the latter had left home before 1973, but Richard and Joan

[62] *Marriage Certificate*
[63] *GRO Index for Q/E March 1908 [Bakewell 7b 937]*
[64] *Electoral Roll 1934*
[65] *Marriage Certificate*
[66] *Information from Mrs Muriel Waters (nee Bragg)*
[67] *GRO Index for Q/E June 1920 [Solihull 6d 1800]*
[68] *Electoral Roll 1945*
[69] *GRO Index for Q/E September 1921 [Solihull 6d 1570]*
[70] *GRO Index for Q/E December 1932 [Birmingham 6d 534]*
[71] *Information from Mrs Diana Mitchell MBE*
[72] *Information from Mrs Patricia Moore (nee Lees)*

remained until December 1979. Both were keen golfers and were members of the Copt Heath Club. Richard was a bank official with Martins Bank[73]. Their telephone number was Solihull 0311. Mrs LEES, now widowed, still lives in Solihull and her son runs a local house maintenance business called Jobs Unlimited[74].

Geoffrey & Moira WYATT arrived in 1980, and are still there today with the same telephone number. They have three daughters, Catherine born on 11 August 1976, Alice born on 7 August 1978 and Lucy born on 29 March 1981. Geoff became a Churchwarden of St Helen's Church in 2002.

### No 9    ENNISCRONE / COMPTON.

The first occupant was George Frederick DOWNES who must have moved into No 9 slightly later than his neighbour Percy Chatterley at No 7, since the first electoral roll on which he appeared was 1908. He named his house *Enniscrone*[75] and had installed a telephone (Solihull 225) before 1924. He had been recorded aged 3 in the 1881 Census at home (29 Alfred Street, Kings Norton) with his two brothers and five sisters. His father Daniel, aged 42 from Warwick, was a whip maker and his mother Agnes (37) came from Lutterworth. George married Katherine Melvin in 1903[76] and they had a son, John Frederick born on 21 December 1903 in Maney Hill Road, Sutton Coldfield. His birth was registered on 26 January, when George was described as a law student.[77].

On 24 June 1911 Joseph Wells sold the freehold of Nos 7 & 9 (overall frontage 22yds 1ft 6ins) for £2,000 to John Smedley Crooke, pawnbroker & jeweller, and Hubert Rowlands, solicitor, of 41 Temple Row, Birmingham, who were the trustees of the late W.H.Wood's estate, and purchased Nos 2, 5, 7, 11 & 13 on the same day. Eight years later, on 26 November 1919, George Downes, by then described as a solicitor, bought the house (frontage 11yds 9ins) from his landlords for £1,150. Mr & Mrs Downes stayed until 1925 but then moved to *Enniscrone*, Blossomfield Road. Before leaving they changed the name of this house to *Compton*.

Ernest George DAVIES, a chartered accountant, of 1 Waterloo Street, Birmingham, bought *Compton* for £1,350 on 18 June 1925. The telephone number was changed to Solihull 254, which by 1932 with four figure numbering became 0254. Ernest had been born on 12 February 1886 and married Lydia Maud Palmer in 1914[78]; they had a daughter Sheila Maud in 1916[79]. At *Compton* they had a servant called Sarah Parker in 1929, who was succeeded a year later by Margaret Josephine Hally and Lily Jennings[80]. Lily Jennings had left by 1931. Mr & Mrs Davies, with Margaret Hally, left in 1934[81]. They moved to 600

[73] *Ibid*
[74] *Information from Mrs Diana Mitchell MBE*
[75] *Kelly's Directory for Warwickshire 1908*
[76] *GRO Index for Q/E June 1903 [Solihull 6d 1157]*
[77] *Birth Certificate*
[78] *GRO Index for Q/E September 1914 [West Bromwich 6b 1671]*
[79] *GRO Index for Q/E June 1916 [Wetherby 9a 202]*
[80] *Electoral Roll 1930*
[81] *Electoral Roll 1934*

Warwick Road, where Lydia died aged 62 on 30 January 1947 and was buried in St Alphege Churchyard on 3 February[82]. Probate for her estate, £3,947-12s was granted to her husband and daughter, now Sheila Maud Whitlock (the wife of David Henry Whitlock). Ernest married secondly Madeleine E.Cook in 1948[83]. The 1967 electoral roll showed them living at 85 Grange Road, Dorridge, where he died aged 86 on 2 November 1972. His estate was worth £22,946. Madeleine continued to live in the Dorridge house.

Described simply as a widow of *Elvet*, St Bernards Road, Olton, Mrs Doris Mary SANDERS bought *Compton* for £1,000 on 31 March 1936. She came with Eleanor Davies who was replaced in 1938 by Lillian Scragg. By 1945 they had been joined by Ellen Angela Morris. Doris SANDERS was a doctor - an anaesthetist at Birmingham General Hospital. Nee Lunn, she had married Edgar Sanders in 1929[84], but the marriage had failed. They had a daughter, Rosemary born in 1930[85], who lived with her mother and was listed on the 1952 electoral roll. Miss Morris was a schoolteacher at Olton Convent[86].The telephone number in July 1949 was Solihull 0891. On 30 December 1948 an application to erect a garage was approved by the local Planning Authority.

On 9 August 1957 Dr Sanders sold the house for £3,725 to Roy Mainwaring DUNSTAN of 202 Marshall Lake Road, Shirley. Mr Dunstan mortgaged the property on the same day to the Halifax Building Society for £2,000, with interest at 6%. The mortgage was redeemed on 23 July 1964 when the Dunstans moved to Snitterfield. Roy & Jean Dunstan gave up using the house name, but retained the 0891 telephone number. Roy was a prosecuting solicitor at Birmingham Magistrates Court, and later became the Secretary of the Stratford-on-Avon Racing Club[87].

Bertie DENT, sales manager, of 48 Lennox Road, North Southsea, Portsmouth, and his wife Pauline Rachel DENT (nee Chamberlain) bought the property on 10 August 1964 for £6,300. On the same day the Dents raised a mortgage of £2,300 at 5% from Kathleen Linington, widow, of Southsea; Lorna Braun of London W8 (the wife of John Braun); and Julian Linington, solicitor, of Portsmouth. This is probably the last example in Ashleigh Road of a 'private' mortgage as opposed to one from a building society or bank. In 1968 the DENTs were joined by Maud DENT, his mother. The latter (born about 1883) died in 1971[88]. The telephone number remained Solihull 0891. Bertie worked in electrical goods. They had a daughter, Rachel born in 1954[89], who became a nurse. On leaving the house the Dents moved to Swanage to run a guest house[90].

John and Evelyn L.LOYNTON from 86 Homer Road, Solihull bought the house on 20 February 1969 for £8,100. They came with their children John, who became a master at

---

[82] *Burial Records of St Alphege Church*

[83] *GRO Index for Q/E March 1948 [Solihull 9c 2223]*

[84] *GRO Index for Q/E December 1929 [Warwick 6d 1825]*

[85] *GRO Index for Q/E December 1930 [Solihull 6d 1167]*

[86] *Information from Mrs Muriel Waters (nee Bragg)*

[87] *Information from Mr George Pemberton*

[88] *GRO Index for Q/E March 1971 [Birmingham 9c 1299]*

[89] *GRO Index for Q/E March 1954 [Surrey Mid E. 5g 273]*

[90] *Information from Mrs Pam Johnson (nee Fox)*

Solihull School, and Averill who also became a teacher. Both have long since left home, but Mr & Mrs Loynton are still in residence today and kindly allowed me access to the deeds of their house. John, senior, who in his younger days was a Football League Referee, worked in the motor trade and was the West Midlands Agent for Lotus Cars for many years before he retired.

### No 11   WESTFIELD / GLENGARTH

Semi-detached with No 13, they are *'similar in plan to 7 & 9 but have been given a completely different first and second floor treatment: the main bedroom windows are pedimented and the second floor gables are rendered, with each gable containing a decorative, diamond shaped plaque. Both houses have the inglenook window and the first floor railing is positioned over the front entrances for security* purposes'[91]. The hallway is similar to No 12 opposite, but on a smaller scale, and it is probable that the same architect designed both houses. The plot for No 11 has a frontage of 11yds 9ins and the standard depth of 80yds 1ft 6ins.

Built about 1905/6, the house's first occupant was John PARTRIDGE who named it *Westfield*[92]. He was a tenant of Joseph Albert Wells, the developer of Ashleigh Road, who did not sell *Westfield* (and *Oakdene* next door) until 24 June 1911. The purchasers, for £2,000 for the pair, were Hubert Rowlands, solicitor, of Temple Row & John Smedley Crooke, pawnbroker & jeweller, of High Street, Birmingham who were the trustees of the estate of the late William Henry Wood, pawnbroker & jeweller, of 37 High Street, Birmingham, who had died on 11 July 1900. The trustees bought Nos 2, 5, 7, 9 & 13 from Mr Wells on the same day.

John PARTRIDGE had been born in 1852/3 in Handsworth, the son of Edward, a butcher from Hunnington (Worcs), and his wife Elizabeth. He married Caroline Beavan, who had been born in 1857/8 at Leintwardine (Herefords), in 1880[93]. The 1881 Census showed them living with his parents – and unmarried sister Anne aged 40 – at 8 Alfred Road, Handsworth, where their daughter Gertrude Mary was born on 2 July that year[94]. John was a bank clerk. Their son, Frederick, was born in 1888[95] also in Handsworth. By the time of the 1901 Census, the family had moved to Solihull where they lived at *Hazeldene* in New Road. John was now described as a bank cashier and his daughter as a student of science. His wife was away on Census night, but the family had a domestic servant. They may have retained a female servant when they moved to Ashleigh Road but, because women did not then have a vote, there was no entry in the electoral roll. However the 1912 roll showed that John Partridge sublet a furnished room on the first floor to Frederick Partridge, possibly his 23 year old son.

In 1916[96] Arthur George SHEPHERD became the tenant and changed the house name

[91] *Ashleigh Road Conservation Area by Simon Herrick*
[92] *Electoral .Roll 1908*
[93] *GRO Index for Q/E September 1880 [Stockport 8a 57]*
[94] *Birth Certificate*
[95] *GRO Index for Q/E June 1888 [West Bromwich 6b 770]*
[96] *Kelly's Directory for Warwickshire 1916*

to *Glengarth*. The Partridges moved across the road to No 20, taking the house name *Westfield* with them. On 30 January 1919 Mr Shepherd bought *Glengarth* from the trustees for £1105. The 1921 Electoral Roll recorded his wife's names as Ellen Maria.

Arthur Shepherd came from a family of cardboard box manufacturers. His father, Ebenezer, who had been born in Aston about 1831, was shown in the 1881 Census as employing 100 people. His mother, Susanna, had been born in Southampton in 1843 and at the time of the Census the family, with two domestic servants, were living at *The Limes,* Victoria Road, Yardley. Arthur was the third son aged 17 and shown as a scholar. His eldest brother, William aged 22, had become an insurance agent rather than enter the family business, but Charles the second son aged 18 had joined the firm – as Arthur would do in due course. He had four younger brothers and a sister.

Arthur married Ellen and had two children. Harold Arthur was born in 1887[97], became a cardboard box manufacturer and from 311 Soho Road married Florence Sophia Wrigley on 17 August 1910 at St James, Handsworth[98]. She was aged 25, the daughter of Elijah Wrigley, an engineer, of 25 Whateley Road, Handsworth. Gladys Dorothy was born in 1894[99] and, from *Glengarth,* married Albert Smart in 1920[100]. Arthur is believed to have become a Governor of Solihull School at some time[101]. Described as a gentleman in the Probate Index of Wills, Mr Shepherd moved to *Medina*, Sharmans Cross, where he died aged 67 on 18 November 1930. Probate for his estate, £17,528-3-5d, was granted to his widow Ellen; son Harold who by that time lived with his wife Florence at 77 Silhill Hall Road; and daughter Gladys. Ellen moved to 13 Lonsdale Road, Leamington, where she died aged 79 on 10 March 1944 worth £9,871-2-11d..

*Glengarth* was sold on 26 March 1923 for £1,700 to Albert VANSTONE, fruit merchant, of 535 Coventry Road, Birmingham. He and his wife, Gwendoline Mary, did not stay long: within six months, and losing £200 plus fees in the process, Albert sold it for £1,500 on 4 October 1923. The VANSTONEs moved to 90 Silhill Hall Road[102] and later to 21 Woodside Way where Albert died aged 70 on 24 October 1972 worth £81,546, and Gwendoline on 30 July 1975 aged 72[103].

The new owners were Charles Thomas CONSTANTINE, gentleman, & Martha Alberta Stanley CONSTANTINE (nee Green), his wife, of *Meadowcroft*, Bakers Lane, Knowle. Thus began the long association of the house with the Constantine family who retained the freehold for 40 years until June 1953. On 5 October 1923 Mr & Mrs Constantine mortgaged *Glengarth* for £500 to Albert Wise, retired die sinker, of Rosalie Street, Birmingham. The interest rate was 5%. They repaid £200 on 27 January 1928 and the remaining £300 on 30 August 1933. By 1928 the telephone had been installed: the number was Solihull 270. On 17 December 1930 Charles Thomas Constantine died aged 70 at Solihull Nursing

---

[97] *GRO Index for Q/E March 1887 [West Bromwich 6b 756]*
[98] *Marriage Certificate*
[99] *GRO Index for Q/E December 1894 [West Bromwich 6b 809]*
[100] *GRO Index for Q/E September 1920 [Solihull 6d 2274]*
[101] *Information from Mr David Turnbull*
[102] *Electoral Roll 1940*
[103] *Burial Records of St Alphege Church*

Home in Station Road[104]. He was then described as formerly of the Stafford Electro Plate Manufacturing Company of Weston Road, Handsworth. Probate for his estate (£747-14-4d) was granted to his widow.

There is no Martha Alberta in the electoral rolls between 1924-1935, but an Alice is listed in each of those years, and this may have been how Mrs Constantine preferred to be known. Otherwise, Alice might have been a daughter but the date of her birth cannot be found; to qualify for the roll, she must have been aged at least 30 in 1924. The Constantines certainly had two sons. (Alfred) Cecil witnessed the mortgage in 1923 and was then described as a metallurgist. He appeared on the electoral roll between 1929-1931 when, in the last quarter of the latter year, he married[105] Edith Mary Tustain of No 12 Ashleigh Road. (Thomas) Stanley had been born in 1894[106] and was listed in the electoral rolls from 1924-1935. Kelly's Directory for 1932 listed Mrs Constantine at *Glengarth*, but the electoral roll showed only Alice and Stanley there. Mrs Constantine went to live at The Desmond Hotel, Kenilworth.

By 1936[107] the house had been let to Albert & Elsie PALEY who came from *Ravenfield*, Warwick Road, but previously[108] had lived at 80 Silhill Hall Road. They remained until early 1945. Their telephone number was Solihull 0861.

Mrs Constantine, now of 37 Victoria Road, Acocks Green, died aged 85 on 28 November 1943 worth £1,551-19-11d. On 22 March 1945 Cecil, her executor, described as a manufacturer of 614 Warwick Road, Solihull, vested *Glengarth* in the ownership of his brother Stanley, now described as a manufacturing jeweller of 42 Westbourne Road, Olton. Stanley and his wife Kathleen moved in, retaining the 0861 telephone number. On 7 December 1951 they mortgaged *Glengarth* for £500 to John Sherman, solicitor, of Four Oaks. The interest rate was 4.5%. Stanley died on 7 November 1952 aged 58 with an estate of £3,805-1-6d. His widow became the owner of *Glengarth* on 27 January 1953 and the following day borrowed a further £250 from John Sherman, still at 4.5%. Kathleen CONSTANTINE, now of Alfington Farm, Ottery St Mary, Devon, sold *Glengarth* on 5 June 1953 for £3,250.

The new owners were James Edward and Marjorie Ethel GIBBS of 10 Pinfold Road, Solihull. James had been born on 11 June 1907 in Solihull and had married Marjorie Apps (born in 1910[109]) in 1938[110]. They lived in the house with their children Richard, who went to Solihull School and appeared on the 1968 electoral roll, and Helen. The telephone number became Solihull 2028. The electoral roll also listed Edgar R B Morris between 1960-64; Suzanne Upton in 1969, and David C.Crampton in 1970: perhaps these were lodgers. James Gibbs died on 18 November 1969 on the way to Birmingham General Hospital. His estate was valued for probate at £10,894 net, on which estate duty of £857 was paid.

---

[104] *Probate Index of Wills*
[105] *GRO Index for Q/E December 1931 [Solihull 6d 1678]*
[106] *GRO Index for Q/E September 1894 [West Bromwich 6b 766]*
[107] *Kelly's Directory for Warwickshire 1936*
[108] *Electoral Roll 1932*
[109] *GRO Index for Q/E December 1910 [W.Bromwich 6b 766]*
[110] *GRO Index for Q/E September 1938 [Meriden 6d 2045]*

David & Diana TURNBULL of 5 Winterbourne Road, Solihull bought the house on 1 October 1970 from Marjorie GIBBS for £8,500. They kindly provided the above information from Conveyances, Assignments & Mortgage Indentures. David taught at Solihull School from 1953, and was its Director of Music for many years until his retirement in 1991. The Turnbulls have three children - James Henry (born 16 May 1968) and Claire Lucy (born 11 December 1970), both of whom are now married; and Charlotte (born 8 May 1976) who is now engaged.

The rear gardens of Nos 3 - 11 all slope away to the east. Unusually, if not uniquely, the garden of this house has been stepped.

### No 13   OAKDENE

Joseph Wells, the developer of Ashleigh Road, retained the freehold of this house until 24 June 1911, when he sold it & No 11 for £2,000 the pair to Hubert Rowlands, solicitor of Temple Row, & John Crooke, pawnbroker & jeweller of High Street, Birmingham, who were the trustees of the late W.H.Wood[111].

Albert Harry SMITH was the first tenant of the house in 1907[112], which he named *'Oakdene'*[113]. He had been born in Handsworth in 1862, the third of five children of Benjamin (a furniture & carpet dealer) and Sophia Smith. By the time of the 1881 Census the family were living at 62 St Peters Road, Handsworth, and Albert was listed as an apprentice brassfounder. The household was reasonably well off with a cook and a housemaid.

On 13 November 1919 Albert, now described as a manufacturer, bought Oakdene from Messrs Rowlands & Crook for £1,105. The following day he mortgaged the property for £750 back to Rowlands & Crook. Interest was 5% pa (increased to 6% on 14 November 1921), payable on 14 May & 14 November. One of the conditions of the mortgage was that Mr Smith insured the property against loss/damage by fire for £1,000 with the Century Insurance Office. Messrs Rowlands & Smith transferred the mortgage, now for £500, on 16 December 1921 to Albert Ernest Apperson, surgeon-dentist, of Gravelly Hill North, Birmingham. Albert Smith repaid the mortgage on 15 May 1933.

Albert remained a bachelor. In 1920[114] his elder brother Sidney, born 1857 in Birmingham and described in 1881 as a furniture & carpet dealer assistant, was also living at *Oakdene*; in 1922 he had been replaced by Eric Wallace; and by 1924 Albert was by himself again. That remained the situation for the next four years. In 1929 Albert was joined by his three unmarried sisters - Marian Sophia (b 1858), Frances Mary (b 1863) & Lillian (b 1874). By 1932 the house had a telephone, Solihull 0911. Tragedy came in 1935: Albert died aged 73 on 21 December (worth £5,014-15-9d), and Marian aged 77 on Christmas Day (£3,392-19-3d). The 1937 electoral roll listed only Frances & Lillian. Frances died aged 80 on 9 March 1944[115]. Lilian alone was left but she did not always live by herself: Mollie

---

[111] *Conveyance*
[112] *Electoral Roll 1907*
[113] *Kelly's Directory for Warwickshire 1908*
[114] *Electoral Roll 1920*
[115] *Title Abstract*

Warren-Codrington was with her in 1945 & 1946; Eric Cowell in 1948; Elizabeth Brown in 1952; and Roselin Bessie Sheasby from 1953 to 1955[116].

Clive Alwyne SILVESTER bought *Oakdene* for £3,250 from Lilian Smith on 5 November 1955. Born in 1927[117], he was the son of Alwyne Thomas & Sybil Kathleen (nee Pope) Silvester of Eastcote Manor, Hampton-in-Arden. Clive married Yvette M.M.Lemasson in 1953[118] and they had a son. Initially they lived with his parents at Eastcote Manor. A month after buying *Oakdene* Clive had K.Bradley Miller, ARIBA, of Devereux House, Coleshill draw up plans for a garage & covered yard. This was duly constructed in 1956. Clive Silvester had an antique shop on the corner of Poplar Road & Warwick Road. He was the brother of Anthony Silvester, who lived with his wife Alexandra at *The Squirrels*, 579 Warwick Road. Anthony, also a local antiques dealer, was said to have considered converting the rundown Solihull Hall for use as a show room when it was up for sale in 1964[119].

Jack Oliver Urban TALLETT, company director, of 33 Rectory Road, Solihull bought the property for £4,750 on 2 February 1959. A week later he raised a mortgage from the National Provincial Bank. His wife's name was Dorothy, and they had two sons, Simon (who appeared on the 1970 electoral roll) and another who was mentally retarded [120], which made Dorothy shy and abrupt. The telephone number became Solihull 1651, which it has remained. On leaving Ashleigh Road the Talletts moved to Wales to run a hotel so that their second son could be employed.

The property was bought for £9,365 on 23 November 1970 by Malcolm LOUGH of 5 Emscote Green, Solihull. He & Anna have occupied the house since then, initially with their three daughters (Suzanah, Kate & Sally), and kindly loaned the deeds to form the basis of the above information.

## No 15   MAVESYN / WOODFORD

'Nos 15 & 17 are another fine pair of 3 storey, semi-detached houses with fenestration very similar to 11 & 13. The gables of 15 & 17 have the full applied timber frame treatment, and bay windows occur in the drawing rooms. Each house also has the fireplace window, and it would seem then that the same architect (in fact E.H.Wigley) designed these three sets of semi-detached houses (7 & 9; 11 & 13; 15 & 17). Nos 15 & 17 are arranged on a plan with a narrower entrance hall than found in the other two pairs.'[121] Joseph Wells sold the 19 yard frontage plot on which Nos 15 & 17 were built for £225 to Samuel Benjamin Barns of The Grange, Solihull on 10 March 1904. Mr Barns became Ernest Wigley's father-in-law when the architect married his daughter Edith on 28 September 1904, and went to live at No 17.

The first occupier was John George WILLIAMS[122], who named the house *Mavesyn*.

---

[116] *Electoral Rolls*
[117] *GRO Index for Q/E December 1927 [Meriden 6d 842]*
[118] *GRO Index for Q/E December 1953 [Meriden 9c 1325]*
[119] *Solihull News 6 April 1966*
[120] *Information from Miss Mollie Bullock*
[121] *Ashleigh Road Conservation Area by Simon Herrick*
[122] *Electoral Roll 1907*

He was still there in 1911, but had been replaced early in 1912[123] by William CHAMBERLAIN, described as a letter cutter[124]. His wife was called Elizabeth[125] and they had a daughter called Edna, born in 1906[126]. They did not stay long before moving to No 4 in July 1912.

The next occupant of Mavesyn was Edward Blakeway BAGOTT who lived in the house for seven years up until about 1919. Born in 1853[127], he became a chemist, like his father. He was shown in the 1881 Census aged 28 and still single at 26 High Street, Dudley with his two sisters, Fanny (16) and Emily (13), his parents being away. He married Agnes Marion Bateman, the daughter of John Bateman auctioneer, on 4 October 1883 at St Thomas, Dudley[128]. Edward died at 78 Pembroke Crescent, Hove on 30 January 1934. Probate for his estate worth £33,648-9s was granted to Henry Pearman Bagott, solicitor, believed to have been his nephew.

By 1920[129] Herbert William & Mary Jane PERIAM (at No 10 from 1910 to 1913) occupied *Mavesyn*. He was a manufacturer of nuts & bolts. Their eldest son, Herbert Bonney Periam, lived with them as did John Bonney, Mary's father. The latter had left by 1923. At this time John Shirley Periam, the second son, and his wife Alice Maud lived in Whitefields Road, although by 1932 they had moved to *Whitefields,* Warwick Road, where they had George Ronald and Audrey Joan Periam living with them. The Ashleigh Road house was empty in 1924 as the senior Periams had gone to live at 58 Sarehole Road, Hall Green.

Up until now all the occupiers had been tenants of Samuel Barns or, following his death on 19 January 1920, of the trustees of his estate. On 31 January 1925 Maurice Herbert HIRST, gentleman, of *Cailima*, Elmdon Road, Marston Green, Warwickshire, bought the house for £1,100 from the trustees. He and his wife, Olive, changed its name to *Woodford*. One of the reasons for this was may have been because there was a *Mavesyn* in Warwick Road[130]. Maurice was the son of John Thomas Hirst, a railway clerk, who had died before he married Olive Mary Pank on 6 September 1913 at the Congregational Church, Westminster Road, Handsworth[131]. She was 27, the daughter of Frank Pank, a leather merchant. Maurice was described as a cashier. He and Olive had a son, John Malcolm born in 1926[132] Maurice died aged only 44 on 1 December 1928 worth £2,777-19-6d.

Olive was listed by herself in 1929, and in 1930 she had a servant Emma Hayward, but the latter had left by 1933. Mrs Hirst lived with her son, John, who was first listed in the 1946 electoral roll. He had left home by 1953, but Mrs Hirst stayed at No 15 until 1958. She never installed a telephone, and indeed remained a tenant of her husband's estate until

---

[123] *Kelly's Directory for Warwickshire 1912*

[124] *Conveyance for No 4*

[125] *Electoral Roll 1921*

[126] *GRO Index for Q/E December 1906 [Aston 6d 336]*

[127] *GRO Index for Q/E September 1853 [Dudley 6c 88]*

[128] *Marriage Certificate*

[129] *Electoral Roll 1920*

[130] *Electoral Roll 1928*

[131] *Marriage Certificate*

[132] *GRO Index for Q/E December 1926 [Barnsley 9c 485]*

17 December 1957 when Ernest Hinchley, her late husband's executor, now of 128 Dorridge Road, Knowle vested Woodford in her name. Witnessed by her son, now a research plant pathologist of 36 Wordsworth Road, Harpenden, Herts, Mrs Hirst sold the property in 1958 for £2,995. At some point she went to live at *The Cottage,* Butcombe near Bristol, where she died on 18 October 1975 leaving £58,925.

The purchaser of *Woodford* on 7 January 1958 was Peter Keith LIVINGSTONE, political agent, of 8 Bridge Road, Worthing. He and his wife Phyllis, who immediately installed a telephone (Solihull 4331), had Julia & Lilian Screeton living with them[133].

On 19 January 1962 *Woodford* was sold for £4,650 to the Rev'd Denis James PAXMAN of 589 Warwick Road. He was the Chaplain at Solihull School from 1956-65. Educated at St Edmund Hall, Oxford (BA 1950, MA 1954), he trained for the priesthood at Ely Theological College and was curate of Bearsted (Kent) between 1953-56. After leaving Solihull, Denis became Warden & Headmaster of St Michael College, Tenbury[134]. His wife was called Mary, and the telephone number of the house became Solihull 2068. Mr Paxman mortgaged the property with the Birmingham Incorporated Building Society, and then on 20 January 1962 took out a second mortgage for £1,395 with the Solihull United Charities at 5%. As they had spare rooms in No 15, Denis & Mary had James Bennett as a lodger plus, for a year from September 1963, Harry R.Rickman. The latter was a master at Solihull School who directed, with great professionalism, its annual musical shows (the orchestra being conducted by David Turnbull of No 11) until his retirement in 1999. In 1965 the lodgers were David Smith & Derek Walker.

Alfred John Gordon & Hilary Jocelyn NEWMAN of 161 Longdon Road, Solihull bought the property for £6,000 on 26 August 1965. Judith H.Cummings (born 7 June 1953), Peter C.A.Cummings (born 16 December 1956) and Mary Cummings (born 22 November 1961), the children of Hilary's first marriage, lived with them. After a career with British Gas, Alf - at the age of 55 - became a non-stipendiary priest at St Peter, Hall Green in 1974. Hilary practised and taught yoga, and was also an Avon Lady[135]. In the evening when we had just moved into No 14 (opposite) in August 1977 Hilary greeted us with a flask of cocoa - very welcome after a tiring and very wet day. The NEWMANs stayed until 1984 when they moved to Leiston (Suffolk); in 1996 they went to Hailsham (Sussex).

They were succeeded by Bruce & Hilary STONE, both teachers, of 10 Reservoir Road, Olton, who bought the house on 14 November 1984. They have Ben & Rachel (twins born on 7 March 1978), and are still there today. They kindly lent the deeds of their house to help compile the above information.

## No 17  KILMORNA
This was the home of the architect, Ernest Homer WIGLEY, who designed a number of houses in Ashleigh Road - certainly Nos 1, 14, 16 & 18; probably this one & Nos 15, 19, 13 & 11, 9 & 7 and 31 & 33; and possibly No 12. Unlike its pair, Kilmorna has a side passageway between the house and its garage, which itself is paired with the garage of

---

[133] *Electoral Roll 1959*
[134] *Crockford's Clerical Directory 1967*
[135] *Information from Harry & Anne Lavery*

No 19. *'Applied timber framing occurs above the doors and with a hipped roof, this little building in itself makes a valuable contribution to the character of Ashleigh Road.'* Ernest WIGLEY's practice was at 121 Colmore Row, Birmingham.

Ernest had been born in 1869[136]. The 1881 Census recorded him as a scholar aged 12, at home in 42 St Bernard's Road, Olton. His father, Reuben Boyce Wigley, 59, was a coffin furniture maker, and his mother Matilda was 42. Ernest was the third of four sons and had four sisters, all of whom had been born in Moseley. In 1901 the family were still in the same house with six children, age range 37 to 27, still unmarried. Ernest was described as an architect & surveyor on his own account – ie neither an employer nor one who was employed. On 28 September 1904 at St Margaret, Olton[137], Ernest (aged 35) married Edith Blanche (32), the daughter of Samuel Benjamin Barns of Solihull Grange. The 1901 Census had shown her at home as the second of five unmarried daughters whose ages then ranged from 35 to 19. The Wigley & Barns families had something in common.

In the same year as Ernest's marriage, his father-in-law bought the land from Joseph Wells for Nos 15, 17 and 19. There were two conveyances, each in the sum of £225 for a frontage of 19 yards: one dated 10 March 1904, the other 23 December 1904. As the conveyance made clear when *Kilmorna* was eventually sold, Mr Barns *erected three messuages on the said lands: the middle one, being semi-detached called Kilmorna with its motor house and outbuildings, was erected partly on the southern portion of the firstly hereinbefore mentioned land and partly on the northern portion of the secondly herinbefore mentioned land.* In fact its curtilege extended by 7 feet into the land covered by the second conveyance.

*Kilmorna* was one of the first 10 houses occupied in the road, in 1907[138]. It still has its original cast iron nameplate. The Wigleys remained in residence until 1925 but never owned the property. The freehold was retained by the trustees of Samuel Barns (who had died on 19 January 1920), of whom Ernest Wigley, his son-in-law, was one. Ernest and Edith had two sons - Terence Barns born in 1905[139], and Brian Homer in 1906[140]. When the family left they went to live at Holbach, Sutton St Nicholas near Hereford, where Edith died aged 70 on 11 December 1942 worth £2,320-0-9d. Her husband and elder son were her executors. Ernest died aged 78 on 13 April 1947 at Pigeon House, Bodenham, Herefordshire, probate of his estate (£2,249-8-3d) being granted to his two sons, who were described as poultry farmers[141].

(William) Foster & Lilian Eliza GOULD bought Kilmorna, with its frontage of 11yds 2ft 6ins, from the trustees of Samuel Barns for £1,200 on 16 January 1925. Foster was the manager of Lloyds Bank in Solihull. He had been born in 1872[142], the eldest son of William Charles & Frances Elizabeth Gould. The family were recorded in the 1881 Census at Brook House, Feckenham (Worcs), where William was described as the senior partner (aged 43) of W.W.Gould & sons, needle & fishhook manufacturers. The family were still there in 1891

---

[136] *GRO Index for Q/E June 1869 [Kings Norton 6c 382]*

[137] *Marriage Certificate*

[138] *Electoral Roll 1907*

[139] *GRO Index for Q/E September 1905 [Solihull 6d 625]*

[140] *GRO Index for Q/E September 1906 [Solihull 6d 659]*

[141] *Probate Index of Wills*

[142] *GRO Index for Q/E December 1872 [Alcester 6d 630]*

*Nos 15, 17 and 19 in 2002. 15 and 17 are a semi-detached pair but No 19 is linked to them by a semi-detached garage. They were designed by E.H.Wigley, who lived in No 17. A slightly wider plot enabled him to have a larger garage and a side passage.*

and Foster, now 18, was described as a bankers' clerk. He married Lilian in 1901[143] and they had two sons, (William) Ronald born in 1902[144] and Henry Alan in 1905[145]. The latter appeared in the 1929 electoral roll, and both had left home by 1934. They also had a servant, Annie Taylor in 1929 and Ruth Mary Smith from 1934 to 1936, but not a telephone until 1955 (Solihull 1743). Lilian died on 17 January 1951 worth £11,008-9-6d. Foster remained in the house and was looked after by Ethel Baker & Mary Harper, although the latter was replaced in 1956 by Roselin Sheasby who had moved from No 13 where she had been looking after Lilian Smith. Roselin Sheasby was in turn replaced by Anne Blackburn in 1958 and by Lucy Weaver in 1962. Foster died aged 91 on 21 March 1964 worth £6,131, his sons being his executors - Ronald was described as a commercial manager and Henry as a chartered surveyor[146].

Dudley Bond LOVE and his wife Anabel Ada of 48 Warwick New Road, Leamington Spa bought the house on 3 September 1964 for £5,750, after he had been appointed Director of Education for Solihull. They retained the 1743 telephone number. Born on 19 July 1914 in London, Dudley was educated at Stratford Grammar School & London University, where

---

[143] *GRO Index for Q/E December 1901 [Kings Norton 6c 809]*
[144] *GRO Index for Q/E December 1902 [Kings Norton 6c 448a]*
[145] *GRO Index for Q/E December 1905 [Kings Norton 6c 396]*
[146] *Probate Index of Wills*

he gained a degree in law. He became a member of Gray's Inn, and joined the Middlesex Yeomanry (TA) in 1938 as the prospect of war loomed. In 1941 he transferred to the Indian Army and was on the staff of the XIVth Army under General Slim; Dudley was promoted to Major in 1944. He married Anabel BOOTH, who was serving in Queen Alexandra's Nursing Service, in 1945. After the war he did not return to the law, but became an education officer in Surrey (SE Division). He was Assistant Education Officer in Berkshire 1954-58 and Warwickshire 1958-63, before coming to Solihull. Dudley served on a number of educational bodies and was Chairman of the Society of Midland Education Officers for two years before his retirement in 1976. He was elected Convenor of the Solihull Social Democratic Party in 1981[147].

Dudley and Anabel - who had a beautiful Aberdonian accent and was known as Bubbles - had two sons (Dudley M. born 31 August 1953, and Timothy born 27 June 1958) and two daughters (Susan, and Charlotte born 27 January 1964). All the children had left home by 1984. Dudley and Bubbles moved on 25 November 1985 to Walberswick (Suffolk) where Dudley died in 1998[148].

They were succeeded by John and Gwyneth JAMES, with Harriet (born 24 September 1975) and Emily (born 22 November 1977), who moved from 19 The Crescent, and are still there today. They kindly loaned the deeds of their house to help compile the above information.

## No 19   CATTERALL / MOORLANDS

Dating from about 1905, it is *one of the most eye catching houses in the road. It is fully timbered above first floor level, and it has a two storey gable to the left and a three story gable to the right, which contains a two storey bay. All this creates a rich but very ordered elevation to the road*[149]. It is not known who designed the house, but almost certainly it was E. H Wigley, as the land was bought by his father-in-law.

Joseph Wells sold this plot for £225 on 23 December 1904 to Samuel Benjamin BARNS, gentleman, of The Grange, Solihull. With a frontage of 19 yards on to *a new road called, or intended to be called, Ashleigh Road*, it had the standard depth of 80yds 1ft 6ins and thus an area of 1529 sq yds. The purchaser, who also bought the land on which Nos 15 & 17 now stand, had to pay 'a proper proportion' of the cost of maintenance of the road until it was taken over by the District Council, and also fence all sides of the property.

Mr Barns' first tenant was Ernest William GOODE[150], and he named the house *Catterall*[151]. Born in 1876, Ernest was recorded in the 1881 Census at home in Greenhill Road, Moseley, with his parents Albert Conrad Goode (a goldsmith) and Marian, five sisters and two brothers. Ernest became a gold chain manufacturer and, aged 29, married Alice Mary Boys Stones at St Thomas, Garstang (Lancashire) on 10 August 1904[152]. Five years

---

[147] *Birmingham Year Book 1989*
[148] *GRO Index for 1998 [Gt Yarmouth 6361B B65B 077 1198]*
[149] *Ashleigh Road Conservation Area by Simon Herrick*
[150] *Electoral Roll 1910*
[151] *Kelly's Directory for Warwickshire 1912*
[152] *Marriage Certificate*

younger than Ernest, she was the daughter of the Rev'd George Boys Stones, the incumbent of that parish. In 1915 Ernest and Alice moved to Herbert Road to a house they also called *Catterall*, where they remained at least until the late 1930s with their son John Alan[153]. Their final move was to 130 Oxford Road, Moseley. Ernest died aged 81 on 18 September 1957 at the Queen Elizabeth Hospital, Birmingham. Probate for his estate (£26,910-18-8d) was granted to Richard Goode, solicitor; John Alan Goode, company director; and Denis Greenway Goode, estate agent.

When Ernest and Alice moved out in 1915, No 19 was occupied by the Misses GOODE, who renamed it *Moorlands*[154]. They were Ernest's maiden aunts, or more precisely step aunts since they were half sisters to his father Albert[155]. The 1920 Electoral Roll gave their full names as Lizzie Mary, Beatrice Violet and Narie (in fact Maria) Corsellis Goode. They had been born at Handsworth in 1854, 1867 & 1869 respectively, and were recorded in the 1881 Census at home (The Moores, Church Lane, Handsworth) with their parents, John Thomas & Sarah Goode, and five brothers (including their half brother, John, born in 1838). Their father was a goldsmith, employing about 50 people. By 1891 their father had died, but Beatrice and Maria still lived with their widowed mother and three brothers (besides a cook and two housemaids) in the same house.

Mr Barns died on 19 January 1920 worth £23,467-15-3d. His executors were his son-in-law Ernest Homer Wigley, architect, who lived at No 17 and Arthur Ernest Ashford, manufacturing jeweller, of 30 Fountain Road, Edgbaston. They sold Moorlands for £3,100 on 25 October 1920 to Harry BILLINGHAM, wine & spirit merchant, of *The Swifts*, Yardley. The property's frontage had been reduced to 16yds 2ft (and hence to an area of 1,342 sq yds) probably when Mr Wigley's house was built taking up slightly more space, with its side passage, than had originally been planned. Since all the properties Nos 15-19 had been owned by Mr Barns, there was no difficulty in doing this. Harry Billingham had been born in 1862[156] at Wollaston, Stourbridge, the second of three sons – and two daughters – of James and Emma Billingham. The 1881 Census showed the family at Laburnam Street, Wollaston, and described Harry was a glass manufacturer's clerk. He married Emma in 1892[157]. Only three months after buying *Moorlands*, Mr Billingham died aged 58 on 14 January 1921 worth £30,016-17-10. Mrs Billingham was listed as the occupier in the 1921 Kelly and shown alone in the 1922 electoral roll.

On 29 March 1926 Mrs Emma Ann BILLINGHAM, widow, now of *Arden Oak*, Warwick Road, sold *Moorlands* for £1,800. It was an immense drop in price from the £3,100 the Billinghams had paid only five and a half years previously. The purchaser was Mrs Elizabeth Ann SUMMERTON, widow, of *Colwall Lodge*, Solihull. Her late husband,

---

[153] *Electoral Roll 1935*
[154] *Kelly's Directory for Warwickshire 1916*
[155] *Albert Conrad had been born on 30 August 1841 at 54 Regent Place, Birmingham, the second son of John Thomas GOODE (born 1813), gold chain maker, and Caroline (nee Abick). Caroline died and John remarried. His second wife was called Sarah and by her he had 4 sons & 3 daughters. The latter never married and came to live in Ashleigh Road*
[156] *GRO Index for Q/E June 1862 [Stourbridge 6c 183]*
[157] *GRO Index for Q/E September 1892 [Dudley 6c 30]*

Charles Richard Summerton, an estate agent, had died on 1 December 1913 worth £3527-1-8d, and under the terms of his will had appointed his wife & son-in-law, John Broadbent Perkins, a company director, to be his trustees. They were to invest the residue of his estate in freehold properties; provide an income for his widow; and on her death divide the estate equally between his son Stanley Bertram Summerton and his daughter Beatrice Bessie, who was married to John Broadbent Perkins. Mrs Summerton bought the property using funds entirely from her late husband's estate, and the day afterwards mortgaged *Moorlands* for £900 to Christopher T.Ward, metal dealer, of 126 Cato Street, Birmingham and Thomas Cross, estate factor of Kirkudbright. Interest was 5% pa, payable on 30 September & 30 March.

Curiously there was no entry for *Moorlands* in the 1926-28 electoral rolls; that for 1929 listed Elizabeth Ann Summerton, Stanley Bertram Summerton (her son) and John Broadbent & Beatrice Bessie Perkins. The 1928 Kelly's Directory had shown John Broadbent PERKINS as the householder, and did so again in 1932, 1936 & 1940. The Perkins had a son (John) Charles Broadbent Perkins born in 1908[158] who was listed at home in the 1930-34 electoral rolls. At times the household had a servant - Minnie Derry in 1931, Mabel Warrington 1933-35, and Edith Annie Pimm 1938-39. In 1936 there was a telephone listed under Mrs Perkins' name, Solihull 1228, and this remains the number today.

Mrs Summerton, known as Bessie, redeemed her £900 mortgage on 1 February 1935, but the next day took out another, for only £150, with Alfred Lattimer, gentleman, of *Lyndale*, Stratford Road, Hall Green. Interest was 5% pa. She died on 14 July 1938 worth only £35-14-2d, with probate being granted to her son & daughter. On 2 February 1939 ownership of the house, together with the £150 mortgage (which they did not redeem until 17 March 1944), was formally conveyed to Stanley SUMMERTON & Beatrice PERKINS. Stanley was an insurance inspector and remained a bachelor. He and Mr & Mrs Perkins remained in the house until 1944.

On 24 March 1944 Clare Margaret ROSS of *Eastnor House*, Stratford-on-Avon, the wife of James Ross, solicitor, bought *Moorlands* for £2,950. James Ross had been born in Edinburgh on 22 March 1913, the son of a surgeon. Educated at Glenalmond & Exeter College, Oxford, he was an assistant prosecuting solicitor in Birmingham from 1941 to 1945 when he became a barrister. He took silk in 1966 and became Recorder of Coventry in 1968. He was appointed a Circuit Judge in 1972 and retired in 1987[159].

James had married Clare Margaret Court-Cox in 1939 and they had a daughter, Heather, born in 1942[160]. The Ross family were keen on pets and had a St Bernard dog and a terrier, besides a more unusual animal. One evening Terence & Muriel Waters from No 10 were sitting in the Ross's drawing room after dinner when Muriel felt something crawling along her shoulder. *'Keep still'* said James *'otherwise it may jump down your front'* It was the pet rat: Muriel was terrified[161]. On another occasion the rat was brought to the Surgery at No 10 for Dr Waters to treat. Mrs Ross was a knowledgeable plantswoman and embellished the

---

[158] *GRO Index for Q/E September 1908 [Solihull 6d 649]*
[159] *Birmingham Year Book 1989*
[160] *GRO Index for Q/E June 1942 [Stratford 6d 1711a]*
[161] *Information from Mrs Muriel Waters [nee Bragg]*

*Original elevation drawing of No 21 by Ewen Harper in 1906.*

garden with many attractive perennials and shrubs. When they left Ashleigh Road, His Honour James & Mrs Ross moved to 45 Avenue Road, Dorridge. He died at Bryn Arden, a nursing home at Claverdon, on 17 August 1996 worth £824,093.

Mrs Ross sold the property on 7 January 1974 for £29,000 to John & June EDWARDS, who came from 109 Links Drive, Solihull. They had two daughters, Sally (born 18 March 1958, who went into public relations and lives in Shirley) and Claire Jane (born 30 November 1959, who became a designer and lives in Chelsea). Mr & Mrs EDWARDS kindly loaned the deeds of their house to form the basis of the above information, before they moved out in November 2001, and later went to London. Their successors were Mark NORTON, a Chartered Surveyor, and Peter SHACKLADY, an interior designer, who moved from 16 Silhill Hall Road.

### No 21   THE CROFT / ALDERLEY

Simon Herrick, Solihull's Conservation Architect, wrote in 1985: *'No 21 was designed in 1906 for Mr John Petrie by Ewen Harper. The house is detached, and is rather unusual in respect of its tile hanging to the front gable. It has a novel flat roofed entrance and the beloved five-sided bay to the drawing room. The China Pantry is noted on the plan as a 'CP', and the larder is under this, approached by a small flight of stairs. Originally there were three bedrooms on the first floor and a further three on the second. The house is not quite as handsome & stylish as one or two of its contemporaries but the bold, semi-circular hood over the front door gives the front elevation the impetus that it needs. Although The Crescent was not built when this house was designed, the plans show that the new road was anticipated and therefore the house was arranged on an 'L' shaped plan in order to present a front to Ashleigh Road and to The Crescent'.*

Whilst the architect's client was John PETRIE, it was Donald Alexander PETRIE, his son, who bought the land from Joseph Albert Wells on 29 September 1906. He paid £350 for the plot with a 24yds 2ft frontage to Ashleigh Road and the standard depth of 80yds 1ft 6ins, a total of 2032 sq yards. The land to the north belonged to Samuel Benjamin Barns, and to the south (reserved for a new road, 14 yards wide) to the executors of R.S.Chattock, who also held the fields to the east. Mr Petrie had to erect a fence within 3 months on 'the back' and south sides.

Kelly's Directory showed John Petrie as the main resident of *The Croft* from 1908 until 1928, before listing Donald from 1932 to 1940. The electoral rolls showed Donald from 1908 by virtue of his ownership of The Croft. John appeared from 1909 until 1929, qualified to vote by occupation (unstated). John Petrie died aged 81 on 12 September 1929. Probate for his estate (£6,935-1-5d) was granted to his son, by then a company director.

Donald Petrie, a bachelor of 36 and described as a works manager, married Dorothy Millicent Palfrey, a telephone operator aged 24, at St Oswald, Bordesley, on 8 June 1917. Born on 3 August 1892, she was the daughter of Thomas E.Palfrey, a shoe last designer. The witnesses were the respective fathers[162]. They had a daughter, Patricia Joan, born in 1918[163]. On 5 January 1921 Donald Petrie applied to The Ministry of Agriculture & Fisheries - on the correct form - to redeem the Tithe Rentcharges under the Tithe Acts 1836-1918. He listed not only his own portion of the old field No 1520 (originally 2316: Gravel Pit Close), but also the areas & monetary apportionment of 12 other residents. It is interesting to note that even at this date Joseph Wells and T.P.Chattock still held land in Ashleigh Road. The full list, in house number rather than the original order, is as follows:

| No | Name | Acre | Rod | Pole | £ | s | d |
|----|------|------|-----|------|---|---|---|
| 1  | R.Lander |  | 3 | 27 |  | 5 | 0 |
| 4  | W.E.Chamberlain |  | 1 | 0 |  | 1 | 5 |
| 8  | T.Casson |  | 1 | 0 |  | 1 | 5 |
| 10 | A.R.Sims |  | 1 | 3 |  | 1 | 6 |
| 12 | G.C.Dean |  | 1 | 23 |  | 2 | 3 |
| 14 | Jas. Cox |  | 2 | 30 |  | 3 | 10 |
| 19 | Exors. of J.B.Barns |  | 2 | 30 |  | 3 | 6 |
| 20 | R.E.Riley |  | 1 | 29 |  | 2 | 5 |
| 21 | D.A.Petrie |  | 1 | 27 |  | 2 | 5 |
| 30 | J.Gloster |  | 1 | 3 |  | 1 | 4 |
| ?  | C.Townley |  | 1 | 0 |  | 1 | 5 |
| ?  | J.A.Wells |  | 2 | 12 |  |  | 9 |
|    | Crooks & Rowlands | 1 | 1 | 4 |  | 7 | 6 |
|    | T.P.Chattock | 1 | 0 | 30 |  | 6 | 0 |
|    |  | 7 | 3 | 20 | 2 | 0 | 4 |

---

[162] *Marriage Certificate*
[163] *GRO Index for Q/E September 1918 [Solihull 6d 1289]*

The money figures do not always cohere with the areas stated, and some of the initials are wrong. Clearly the list is incomplete and the names may be only those with whom Donald Petrie was in contact. The application was returned by The Ministry on 6 July, stating that the tithe had to be redeemed on the whole of the field, not just part of it. Eventually all the residents must have agreed that this should take place, as on 26 November 1924 Mr Petrie received a demand for £3-16-6d (ie much higher than his original calculation of 2s-5d). It is interesting to note that Mrs Zair of No 3 paid £2-7-4d on 6 June 1925 to The Ministry to redeem her portion of the tithe.

On 12 December 1932 Donald Petrie, described as a manufacturer, *desirous of making provision for his wife Dorothy Millicent Petrie* signed a Deed of Gift to her. *Now this deed witnesseth that for the purpose of effectuating the said desire and in consideration of the natural love & affection of the said Donald Alexander Petrie for his wife....(he) conveys that piece or parcel of land situate in & fronting to Ashleigh Road...together also with the messuage or dwellinghouse & outbuildings thereto belonging now erected....and known as The Croft, and now in occupation of Donald Alexander Petrie.*

The Petries had a telephone by 1928[164] - Solihull 376 - which became 0376 with the introduction of four figure numbering in 1931. From 1930 Donald & Dorothy had a living-in servant, Susan Hamer, who stayed with them at least until 1935.

Plans dated 13 August 1954 were drawn up by Philip Skelcher & Partners of 17 Poplar Road, Solihull to create a first floor flat and downstairs bathroom. The specification was dated October, and a pencilled note records the contract as £785. The work was carried out and from Saturday 16 July 1955 Catherine Clucas occupied the furnished flat. The rent was £4-4s per week payable in advance. A tenancy agreement was signed on 6 August, the tenure being quarterly from 29 September. Catherine Clucas had lived with her husband in Silhill Hall Road before being widowed[165].

Donald Petrie was a keen numismatist. He died on 7 June 1957, aged 76. Probate for his estate (£3092-4s) was granted to his widow & the Midland Bank.

Mrs PETRIE sold a small triangle in the south west corner of her land to Solihull Council for 1s on 16 December 1958 to improve the sight lines on The Crescent/Ashleigh Road corner. More importantly on 30 October 1962 she sold, price unstated, 685sq yds of her rear garden, having a frontage of 80ft the The Crescent, to George Henry Lavender for the erection of a dwellinghouse (No 42 The Crescent).

On 20 September 1973 Dorothy Petrie died at 3 St Bernards Road, Olton. Her Will of 21 April 1972 appointed her daughter Patricia Joan Robinson & Roland D.W.Evans (solicitor, of 6 Herbert Road, Solihull) as executors. Mrs Robinson's address was given as 158 Foxley Road, Purley. As Frederick & Florence Robinson had lived at No 20 Ashleigh Road for 20 years up to 1951 before moving to 126 Foxley Lane, Purley, research was undertaken to establish whether any son they might have had, had married the girl opposite before taking her off to live in Purley. It was discovered that Patricia Joan Petrie, aged 21, had married Laurence Brian Robinson, civil engineer (23) on 3 September 1939 at St Alphege, Solihull[166].

---

[164] *Kelly's Directory for Warwickshire 1928*
[165] *Information from Mrs Diana Mitchell MBE*
[166] *Marriage Certificate*

But his father was called Lawrence and was also a civil engineer, whereas Frederick John Robinson of No 20 was a works manager. The declaration of war on the morning of that wedding must have cast a shadow over the reception.

Patricia ROBINSON formally became the owner of No 21 on 24 October 1974. Catherine Clucas was still the tenant of 21A, the first floor flat, and remained there until the end of 1978[167]. Her telephone number was 705 2342. The rest of the house was now let to Philip M.Banner & Sylvia Wardle[168], and then to Donald G.Wyatt & Brenda M.Palmer[169]. Mrs Robinson, now of 95 Woodcote Valley Road, Purley sold the house for £22,000 on 17 January 1978 to Chambers & Guest Ltd. of 614 Stratford Road, Sparkhill. This was a husband & wife property development company, who promptly mortgaged the property to The Midland Bank.

In August 1980 David & Jane BRIGGS purchased the house, which they renamed *Alderley*, after their previous home in Alderley Edge, Cheshire. They kindly lent the property deeds to form the basis of the above information. They have two daughters - Sarah (born 1 August 1968) and Karen (born 8 June 1970), both of whom now live in London. David was a senior manager with Lloyds Bank before his retirement, and has been Churchwarden of the Parish of Solihull since 1994, having been pro-warden of St Alphege before that.

---

[167] *Electoral Roll 1978*
[168] *Electoral Roll 1975*
[169] *Electoral Rolls 1976-1978*

# 5. HOUSES 2 TO 20

## No 2     MANTON

*'Nos 2 & 4, dating from about 1905, are handed versions of the same house. Each is detached but has a semi-detached garage. This phenomenon of the handed pair, with semi-detached garages, occurs virtually opposite at Nos 3 & 5. All this must have been carefully thought about at the time. The arrangement is obviously an interesting piece of suburban planning but on a more mundane level is a cheap way of designing two houses virtually for the price of one. Each house is predominantly of brickwork with a gabled three storey bay. Looking, for instance, at No 2: on the left hand side of the door is a very narrow splayed projecting window which rises to the bedroom. On the right hand side of the door is a full sized bay window to the drawing room and bedroom above; with an oriel window in the gable at second floor level. Each house features casement windows (some with stained glass) and a string course of brickwork at first floor level with a relieving arch just visible below the oriel. This latter feature is both structural and decorative.'[1]*

The construction date is more likely to have been 1908 since that was when No 4 was built by Baker & Warr of Birmingham, and the earliest record of the first occupant in No 2 was in 1910. But Joseph Wells, the developer of Ashleigh Road, retained the freehold of this house, whereas he had sold the plot for No 4 in 1907, and some others even earlier. The first tenant was John Thomas SPRINGTHORPE[2], a solicitor, who had been born at Manton (Rutland) in 1851. He married Edith Fanny Adkins (born 1860) in 1880[3], and the 1881 Census showed the couple at 12 Stratford Road, Aston. They had a daughter, Helen Edith, born in 1884[4] and a son, Gerald William, born on 6 September 1887 in Park Road, Moseley[5]. The Springthorpes named the house *Manton* from John's birthplace. He sublet a furnished room on the first floor to his son[6], who by 1923 was living at *Southside*, Warwick Road[7], and had become a solicitor like his father. John and Edith moved to Herbert Road in 1915[8], and at some point later moved to *Cotswold*, Ramsgate Road, Broadstairs where John died on 17 January 1925. Probate for his estate (£3,565-11-8d) was granted to his son.

The second tenant of *Manton* was Alexander Graham SMITH[9]. Samuel FOSTER became the next tenant about 1918.

---

[1] *Ashleigh Road Conservation Area by Simon Herrick*
[2] *Electoral Roll 1910, which mistakenly listed his first name as Joseph*
[3] *GRO Index for Q/E June 1880 [Aston 6d 420]*
[4] *GRO Index for Q/E March 1884 [Kings Norton 6c 429]*
[5] *Birth Certificate*
[6] *Electoral Roll 1912*
[7] *Electoral Roll 1923*
[8] *Electoral Roll 1915*
[9] *Kelly's Directory for Warwickshire 1916*

*Nos 4 and 2 in 2002. A handed pair built by Baker and Warr about 1908. Note the garden walls and modern lamp post.*

On 24 June 1911 Mr Wells had sold the freehold for £1,012-10s to John Smedley Crooke, pawnbroker & jeweller, of 37-38 High Street, Birmingham and Hubert Rowlands, solicitor, of 41 Temple Row, Birmingham. On the same day Mr Wells also sold Nos 7 & 9 and 11 & 13 for £2,000 each pair, and No 5, to Crook & Rowlands. They were the Trustees of the will dated 20 December 1898 of William Henry Wood (died 11 July 1900), which empowered them to invest trust monies in freehold land in Great Britain & Ireland. The plot had a frontage of 15 yards to Ashleigh Road and a depth of 80yds 1ft 6ins, making an area of 1207 sq yds. The purchasers had to keep the fence on the north & west sides in good repair. It is interesting to note that Rowlands & Co were Joseph Wells' own solicitors, whom he used for all his property transactions in Ashleigh Road.

The trustees in turn sold *Manton* on 4 March 1919 for £1125 to Samuel FOSTER, coal merchant, who was already living in the house. The next day he mortgaged the property back to the trustees to secure £600. The interest rate was 5% pa, payable half yearly on 5 September & 5 March. On 20 December 1920 Dorothy Perkins, spinster, of *The Cottage*, Stoke near Coventry, became the mortgagee instead of the trustees. The sum was increased to £800 and the interest rate went up to 6% pa. This mortgage was redeemed on 29 December 1922. But only five weeks later the property was mortgaged to The London Joint City & Midland Bank Ltd to provide banking facilities and credit to Samuel Foster & his eldest son trading as Thomas Foster & Sons at 14 New Street, Birmingham. This was confirmed on 18 September 1930 after the bank's name had been simplified to The Midland Bank. The arrangement ended on 9 January 1945.

Samuel Foster had been born in 1868[10], the fourth son of Thomas & Ellen Foster. The family was listed in the 1881 Census at 19 St Mark's Street West, Birmingham. Thomas, aged 40, was a smith at a factory, and had six sons and three daughters. In his turn Samuel and his wife, Annie Elizabeth Sproston, whom he had married in 1890[11], had six children. Their eldest son, Horace Samuel Sproston Foster born 1892[12] was with them in 1920[13]; after he had married he lived at No 7 from 1934 to 1952. John Sproston and Neville Thomas were twins, born in 1905[14]: the former was listed in the electoral roll from 1926-31, and the latter from 1926-30 and again in 1945. Percy Allen, Norah Elizabeth and Grace Winifred made up the family. By 1924 there was a telephone in the house, Solihull 93, which was one of only nine in the road. The telephone number became 0093 when 4 figure numbers were introduced in 1931. The Fosters did not generally have a living-in servant although Dorothy Drew was recorded in 1929; Ivy Orzam in 1939; and Helen Nosworthy in 1946-47[15]. By 1945 Annie Foster had disappeared, maybe she had died, and Dorothy D.Foster was listed for that year only.

On 7 March 1945, by a deed of gift, Samuel Foster gave *Manton* to his son, Percy Allen Foster, of *The Cottage*, Howe Green, Great Hollingbury, Bishops Stortford; and daughters Norah Elizabeth Higgs of Hatton Rock, Stratford-on-Avon; and Grace Winifred Norton of 51 Canterbury Avenue, Fulwood, Sheffield, in equal shares. Samuel continued to live in the house until he died aged 78 on 8 March 1947. Probate for his estate (£1,363-1-4d) was granted to his eldest son, Horace, described as a coal merchant, and to his fourth son, Percy, described as a manager.

George Spencer PEMBERTON of 15 Stonor Park Road, Solihull bought *Manton* on 17 July 1947 for £4,300. The telephone number became Solihull 2011 on his arrival, and so it remains today. Born in January 1905 and educated at Dulwich College, George's first job was with the Ardath Cigarette Company (which made the 555 State Express brand) in Worship Street, London. At £3 per week George was well paid, but his father disapproved of cigarettes and secured him a post with The Phoenix Assurance Company in King William Street. George was mortified to find that his salary would be only £70 a year. One day he rushed out of the office, fell down some steps on to the pavement, and knocked over a young man. This turned out to be an old school friend whom he had not seen for several years. The latter worked for the Bank of England earning £170 pa, so George persuaded The Master of Dulwich to write to a Director of The Bank, and secured a job there. In October 1929 the Bank moved George to its Birmingham branch, and in 1932 he married (Helen) Mary Lamplaugh of Acocks Green. They had a son, John Spencer (born 10 April 1936) who became a lawyer, married and had two sons and now lives in Mirfield Road.

[10] *GRO Index for Q/E June 1868 [Aston 6d 252]*
[11] *GRO Index for Q/E September 1890 [Aston 6d 572]*
[12] *GRO Index for Q/E December 1892 [Kings Norton 6c 386]*
[13] *Electoral Roll 1920*
[14] *GRO Index for Q/E March 1905 [Kings Norton 6c 398]*
[15] *Electoral Rolls*

The Pembertons stayed in *Manton* for 14 years until 1961, when George was promoted to be Sub Agent of the Bank of England at Liverpool. On his retirement he and his wife returned to the Midlands. Now a widower, George lives (2002) in Abbeyfield, Hampton Lane.

John Barry JOHNSON of Flat 2, 14 Park Road, Solihull, bought *Manton* on 23 August 1961 for £4,500. He came with his wife Pamela and two children, Paul (born 25 January 1957) and Victoria (18 June 1960), both of whom are now married. John was a director of a retail greengrocery business in Birmingham. The Johnsons ceased to use the house name. John died on 27 November 1992, but Pam continues to live in the house and kindly loaned its deeds on which part of the above account is based.

## No 4    THE CHALET / St JOSEPHS / ARDENHOLME

On 21 February 1907 Joseph Albert Wells of Newtown Row, Birmingham, who developed Ashleigh Road, sold the plot on which this house now stands to Edgar Baker & George Warr, builders, both of Sampson Road, North Camp Hill, Birmingham for £211-6-3d. The size of the plot was 15yds frontage and the 80yd 1ft 6ins depth common to all Ashleigh Road properties, amounting to 1207 sq yds. The land to the north (ie No 2) was still owned by the vendor; to the west by the executors of the late Richard Chattock; and to the south (ie No 6) by Edward Taylor. One of the conditions of the sale was that the purchasers had to erect within three months a good and substantial boundary fence not less than 5ft and not more than 7ft high on the west and northern sides.

Messrs Baker & Warr built the house in 1907/8, and rented it out. The first tenant was William PRIEST[16], and he called it *'The Chalet'*. On 28 October 1910 Messrs Baker & Warr mortgaged *The Chalet* to Mrs Eliza Elizabeth Deakin, widow, of *Strencliffe* (No 33), Ashleigh Road, for £550 The interest rate was 4%. On 14 February 1912 George Warr died: his will (dated 31 March 1910) appointed his son Denis William Warr as his trustee.

William Edward CHAMBERLAIN, letter cutter, of *Mavesyn* (No 15) Ashleigh Road bought *The Chalet* on 11 July 1912 for £700. He paid £550 direct to Mrs Deakin and £150 to Edgar Baker, builder, of Ladypool Road, Birmingham and Denis W. Warr, plumber, of 180 Bradford Street, Birmingham. William Chamberlain moved from across the road with his wife Elizabeth[17] and lived in *The Chalet* for 18 years. They had a daughter Edna born in 1906[18] who appeared on the 1929 electoral roll. They never installed a telephone – despite the growing fashion in the 1920s. On 14 February 1930 Mr Chamberlain mortgaged *The Chalet* to The Birmingham Incorporated Building Society for £800. The interest rate was 5%. The Society had a system of fortnightly repayments of capital/interest in respect of the number of shares granted by the transaction. In this instance for 80 shares Mr Chamberlain had to repay £2-10s fortnightly starting from 18 February 1930.

On 10 May 1930 William Chamberlain sold *The Chalet* to Mary Agnes CLARKSON, the wife of William Joseph Clarkson, chartered accountant, of 13 Plough & Harrow Road, Edgbaston for £1,375. The first thing that Mrs Clarkson did was to rename the house

---

[16] *Kelly Directory for Warwickshire 1912*
[17] *Electoral Roll 1921*
[18] *GRO Index for Q/E December 1906 [Aston 6d 336]*

*St Josephs*; and the second was to mortgage the property on 12 May for £950 with The Birmingham Incorporated Building Society. The interest rate was 5%, but she had to repay £2-19s fortnightly from 19 April for 995 shares. On 10 July 1931 Mrs Clarkson's mortgage was transferred to The Midland Bank; it was discharged on 27 May 1932. By 1930 the house had a telephone (Solihull 0769). The 1931 Electoral Roll listed Edmund Leopold Lauze living with the Clarksons.

Kate Phoebe FLORANCE, widow, of *Oakfield*, Warwick Road, Olton bought the property from Mrs Clarkson for £1,400 on 28 May 1932. She changed its name to *'Ardenholme'*, and lived there with her son Thomas Roderick and her companion Laura Gertrude Benger[19]. But her sojourn was less than 18 months as she died aged 72 on 26 October 1933 worth £15,032-17-8d. Her executors (appointed by a codicil dated 25 May 1928 to her will of 2 September 1909) were her sons John Barber Florance, motor engineer, of *Combe Gate*, 414 Warwick Road, Solihull and Thomas Roderick Florance, commercial traveller, of Buckley Green Farm, Henley-in-Arden. They sold *'Ardenholme formerly known as The Chalet'* on 10 May 1934 for £1,175. It is of interest to note that John Florance's daughter, Gloria, still lives in Solihull.

The purchaser was Oliver Esmond KIRK, cycle manufacturer, of 21 George Road, Solihull. On 11 May 1934, the day after he bought the property, he mortgaged it to Joseph Howard Kirk (possibly his father), cycle manufacturer, of The Grange, Shirley for £1,100. The interest rate was 4%, and the mortgage was repaid on 22 November 1940. Mr Kirk, who became a commercial traveller, lived in the house for nearly 29 years with his wife Barbara, nee Buxton. They had two daughters, Anne D. born in 1932[20] and Claire B. born in 1937[21]. The girls attended The Tree School in Warwick Road before it moved to Station Road, Knowle, as did Margaret Hardaker of No 14 and Jean Robinson of No 20[22]. Anne married Frederick J.Edwards in 1955[23] and lives in Norfolk[24]. Claire married Paul M.Burley, an architect, in 1959[25] and they now live in Dorridge. Mrs Kirk was a Governor of Malvern Hall School, and did much - as did her husband - to ensure the preservation of the Manor House in Solihull High Street[26].

The Kirks installed a telephone on arrival and its number was Solihull 1385, which it remains today. In 1938 they had a servant, Delilah Beatrice Knott, but she was replaced by Evelyn Jones the following year. Mary Wylde lived with them in 1946-48, and Frederick & Anne Edwards in 1956-59. Mr Kirk died aged 55 on 22 February 1963 worth £26,298-18-8d, but his widow remained there until 30 September 1966 when she sold *Ardenholme* for £8,500.

Peter Charles BILSON, a Barclays Bank official, and Margaret Elise (nee Bauman) his wife, from 13 Vale Road, Wilmslow, Cheshire were the purchasers. They had married in

---

[19] *Electoral Roll 1933*
[20] *GRO Index for Q/E September 1932 [Solihull 6d 1208]*
[21] *GRO Index for Q/E September 1937 [ Solihull 6d 1316]*
[22] *Information from Mrs Diana Mitchell MBE*
[23] *GRO Index for Q/E June 1955 [Solihull 9c 1805]*
[24] *Information from Miss Mollie Bullock*
[25] *GRO Index for Q/E September 1959 [Solihull 9c 2432]*
[26] *Information from Mr George Pemberton*

1946[27] and had two sons and a daughter. David P. was born in 1947[28], appeared on the 1968 electoral register, and went to Cambridge University but later had a breakdown. Martin became a veterinary surgeon. The daughter's name was Susan[29]. After less than five years, the Bilsons moved in 1971 to *The Hoo,* Brockhill Road, West Malvern, but on 17 January 1974 they were involved in a car accident on the way to Stratford-on-Avon: Peter died immediately and Margaret on 30 May. Their estates were £7,452 and £61,723 respectively.

The house was sold on 3 May 1971 for £12,300 to George Kay Walker & Jean Allan ARKIESON of 25 Ravenscroft Road, Solihull, but originally from Scotland. They had two adopted children. Bessie J Finnie (possibly Jean's mother) lived with them from 1973 to 1975[30]. George worked in local government, but after only four years was moved to Edinburgh.

Peter & Dallin CHAPMAN, who kindly provided the above information from the Conveyances & Mortgage Indentures, bought the house in 1975. They have three children - Marcus (born 5 December 1965), Richard (born 16 July 1968) and Joanna (born 16 September 1972, who married the Rev'd. Gavin Knight, curate of Solihull in St Alphege Church, on 22 July 2000). Mr & Mrs Chapman moved to Stratford-on-Avon in August 2002 and were succeeded by Mr & Mrs Lewis and their three children.

### No 6   BRANSFORD / ASHBOURNE

This has *'the full mixture of Ashleigh Road ingredients: brickwork, render & applied timber framing; casement windows, leaded lights & stained glass. The house occurs within a run of predominantly brick & render houses and so provides a dramatic contrast. Nevertheless it fits comfortably and is assembled with a skill and flair with which we have become so familiar. It was built around 1905'*[31].

The first occupant was Mrs TAYLOR[32], the wife of Edward TAYLOR, and she named the house *Bransford.* The next, by 1916, was Frederick W.WARD, although he and his wife, Edith Maud, had moved to *Haddon,* Warwick Road by 1921. Their successor at *Bransford* appears to have been Harold Rigby WHITMORE[33], but in 1925 he moved to *Lattiford House,* Birmingham Road.

By May 1929[34] Charles Sydney Herbert CLARKE and his wife Eleanor Gladys, nee Blackham, were in residence, and stayed until after 1955. They had married in 1912[35] and their son, Charles Peter, had been born in 1913[36]. They did not have a telephone until October 1937 when Solihull 1487 was installed, but listed under their son's name; nor did

---

[27] *GRO Index for Q/E June 1946 [Uxbridge 3a 455]*

[28] *GRO Index for Q/E March 1947 [Amersham 6a 553]*

[29] *Information from Mrs Pam Johnson (nee Fox)*

[30] *Electoral Rolls*

[31] *Ashleigh Road Conservation Area by Simon Herrick*

[32] *Kelly's Directory for Warwickshire 1908 & 1912*

[33] *Electoral Roll 1924*

[34] *Electoral Roll 1929*

[35] *GRO Index for Q/E June 1912 [Aston 6d 416]*

[36] *GRO Index for Q/E March 1913 [Aston 6d 797]*

*Nos 6 and 8 in 2002. Note the new porch of No 6 and the central first floor extension of No 8.*

they ever seem to have living-in servants. The electoral rolls for 1934-39 showed their son, that for 1945 Charles & Margaret Massey, and that for 1950 Florence Sophia Clarke who may have been Charles Sydney's sister. Kate Moran lived with them from 1946, Julia Moran arrived in 1948 and Mary Moran joined them in 1950: these seem to have been the Morans who lived at No 32 between 1924 until before 1945. Mr & Mrs Clarke were by themselves in 1955, the year in which they moved to *Braeside,* Longdon Lane, Galmpton, Brixham. Unfortunately after only a few weeks in their new home, Charles died on 26 November 1955. Probate for his estate (£2,347-9-11d) was granted to his widow.

By 1956 the occupants were William Lewis & Thelma Joyce PEART. Harry & Elsie Coombes, lived with them, but Harry died aged 78 on 28 November 1957 at Solihull Hospital. Probate for his estate (£475-16-3d) was granted to his widow. The Pearts appear to have had lodgers since Angela Smith was listed as living in the house in 1958, Dorothy Spenny in 1959, James F. Sharpe in 1960-65, and Anthony & Gloria Rees in 1962-67. The 1960 telephone directory no longer showed a number for the house. The Pearts and Elsie Coombes were in residence until 1969. By February 1970 John & Ruth BUTCHER lived in the house, but John left his wife in 1974. Ruth, a swimming instructor[37] stayed on with her children Joan, Richard and Lynne, the last being born on 1 August 1961.

---

[37] *Information from Mrs Pam Johnson (nee Fox)*

In 1981 Martin & Gwendoline DOLIN were the occupants. Peter BARTLE, a dentist, and Elizabeth ROOTKIN came in October 1983, and married in 1984[38]. They restored the house which had become run down, and named it *Ashbourne*. Each has children from previous marriages, viz Chloe Bartle (b 24 February 1975), Virginia Rootkin (b 30 March 1975), Jethro Bartle (b 9 May 1976) & Robin Rootkin (b 10 August 1976).

## No 8    WHITECLIFF

The first occupant of the house in 1908, which he named *Whitecliff,* was Thomas CASSON[39], and he remained there until 1921[40]. His wife was called Grace Edith[41]. After leaving *Whitecliff,* they moved to 20 Willes Road, Leamington. Grace died aged 72 on 7 October 1924 at Ashwood House, Kingswinford. Probate for her estate, £3,269-5-4d, was granted to Lydia Gordon Allinson and Maud Irene Taylor, widows.

William & Helen ROBINSON had arrived before October 1924[42]. They had a daughter, Winifred Helen (known as Win), born in 1907[43] who appeared in the electoral rolls from 1929 to 1934. She married Ronald Alfred Williams in 1933[44], and went to live at 97 Silhill Hall Road where they stayed for many years[45]. In 1930 *Whitecliff's* telephone number was Solihull 241, which became 0241 the following year with the introduction of four figure numbering. No connection has been found between William & Helen and the Robinsons who lived at No 20 from 1931 to 1951. William died aged 76 on 21 February 1949 at The Hospital, Solihull. Probate for his estate of £5,282-9s was granted to his widow. Helen continued to live in the house[46] by herself and then moved to her daughter & son-in-law's house. She died on 20 October 1963 at 6 Worcester Street, Stourbridge, worth £1,026-15-2d, her daughter being her executor. William & Helen share a tombstone in St Alphege Churchyard.

By 1960 Claude Neville WHITE, known as Nev, had become the owner. He was an architect with a practice at 190 Broad Street, Birmingham, and was the designer in 1958 of the Chapel of Solihull School, of which he was an old boy. He had married Joy(ce) E Cheatle in 1933[47], and they had a son John N, born in 1941[48], who was listed in the 1963-65 electoral rolls. Joy went everywhere on her bicycle[49]. Their telephone number was Solihull 2931, and this remains the number today.

Keith & Ann FOSTER arrived about 1970 with Giles (born 29 June 1967), Carey (b 31 August 1968) & Emma (b 29 August 1970). A Chartered Accountant, Keith went to Solihull

---

[38] *GRO Index for 1984 [Solihull S. 0584 34 0138]*
[39] *Kelly's Directory for Warwickshire 1908*
[40] *Kelly's Directory for Warwickshire 1921*
[41] *Electoral Roll 1920*
[42] *Electoral Roll 1924*
[43] *GRO Index for Q/E December 1907 [Solihull 6d 593]*
[44] *GRO Index for Q/E December 1933 [Solihull 6d 1883]*
[45] *Information from Mrs Diana Mitchell MBE*
[46] *Electoral Rolls 1950-58*
[47] *GRO Index for Q/E September 1933 [Cheltenham 6a 1215]*
[48] *GRO Index for Q/E September 1941 [Bathavon 5c 1440]*
[49] *Information from Mrs Muriel Waters (nee Bragg)*

School and became President of the Old Silhillians Association in 1977. He was also much involved with the Shirley Round Table, and was its Chairman in 1973.

**No 10    CREDITON**
This house was designed in July 1906 by Hipkiss & Stephens of 24 Martineau Street, Birmingham. Their client was William PEARCE who was described as a manufacturer and lived at *Leighcourt*, Warwick Road[50]. He never moved into No 10 which was clearly an investment. He died in 1915 aged 68[51]. The drawings show several changes in the design before it was finalised. The most obvious were the Drawing Room bay window on the left (two storey) side of the house which was originally planned to be flush, and the omission of the originally planned cellar. *'The three storey gabled bay to the right of the front has been built as originally designed. However, the house is rendered from first floor level, whereas the drawings show rendering only to the second floor gable. The junction between the rendering and the brickwork has been achieved by a moulded timber render-stop carried on shaped brackets. This house is unusual in one very special respect: the main entrance is actually a single storey side entrance. Elsewhere in the street, the houses are really designed around the front entrance, which is given obvious prominence and status. Here the large entrance hall and main staircase are relegated to the back of the house.'*[52]. The house was built by Bragg of Solihull[53].

In 1912 the house was named *Crediton* and its occupant was Herbert William PERIAM[54]. The 1910 & 1911 Electoral Rolls recorded him as living simply in Ashleigh Road. Herbert had appeared, aged 30, in the 1881 Census living with his wife Mary (27) & two sons (Herbert B. aged 2 & John S. aged 1) at *Jessamine Villa*, Solihull. He was described as a maker of nuts & bolts, employing 10 men, 9 boys & 6 women/girls. In 1901 the family were living in Lode Lane and had been augmented by a daughter, Charlotte, aged 18. John Bonney, Mary's widowed father aged 68, a retired bolt manufacturer, was living with them. They were still in Lode Lane in 1905[55] and probably came to No 10 Ashleigh Road about 1908. By 1914 they had moved to Warwick Road, but by 1920 had returned to Ashleigh Road (No 15) where they stayed for 4 years. Clearly they liked moving frequently! In their last years they lived at 58 Sarehole Road, Hall Green, where Herbert died aged 76 on 30 July 1927. Probate for his estate of £1,608-0-2d was granted to his widow and his second son John Shirley Periam, merchant. Herbert's company prospered making bolts, rivets & screws in Floodgate Street, Birmingham: it still exists and trades now from 2 Gopsal Street, Birmingham.

In 1916 Frank Cooper COLLINS lived at *Crediton*[56]. He had been born in 1883[57] and became a manufacturing jeweller like his father, Walter Henry Collins. Frank married

---

[50] *Electoral Rolls 1902 & 1912*
[51] *Burial Records of St Alphege Church*
[52] *Ashleigh Road Conservation Area by Simon Herrick*
[53] *Information from Mrs Muriel Waters (nee Bragg)*
[54] *Kelly's Directory for Warwickshire 1912*
[55] *Electoral Roll 1905*
[56] *Kelly's Directory for Warwickshire 1916*
[57] *GRO Index for Q/E December 1883 [Meriden 6d 423]*

Elizabeth Hughes on 18 October 1909 at Eglwys Rhos parish church near Llandudno. Aged 22, she was the daughter of Samuel Hughes of Abbey Road, Llandudno, a company secretary. Sadly Frank died young. *The Birmingham Post* for Monday 17 March 1919 carried the following notice '*COLLINS. On 14th inst, Frank Cooper, dearly beloved husband of Elizabeth Collins, at Crediton, Ashley* (sic) *Road, Solihull in his 36th year. Funeral at St Giles, Nether Whitacre 2.30 today*'. Probate for his estate of £9,364-16-2d was granted to J.H.Freeman druggist and Francis Jubal Reynolds Esq., JP, gentleman.

The Electoral Roll for 1921 listed Frank Harold SIMS and his wife Caroline Mary (nee Poole), and they remained in the house until after World War II. In 1928 they had a telephone Solihull 108, which by 1932 had become Solihull 0108, and this amazingly remains the number to this day. They had married in 1906[58]. Their eldest son Harold Walter was born in 1907[59] and was shown in the 1929 & 1930 electoral rolls; the latter list also included Hilda Annie Lloyd, presumably a servant. She had been replaced by October 1933 by Mary Elizabeth Markham. That electoral roll also showed their daughter Ethel May, who had been born in 1909[60], and their second son William Frank, born in 1912[61] By 1939 the children and servants had left, but Mr & Mrs Sims stayed until 1947, when they sold it for £6,000[62]. They moved to 7 Gregory Road, Stratford-on-Avon, where Frank died on 24 January 1948 worth £17,930-18s. Caroline then returned to Solihull to live at 11 Dovehouse Lane. She died on 22 May 1956 at Calthorpe Nursing Home, 4 Arthur Road, Edgbaston. The executors of her £6,451-11-1d estate were her two sons, described as agricultural engineers.

Dr (Kenneth) Terence WATERS and Muriel Beatrice (nee Bragg), his wife, lived in the house from 1947 until 1962 with their two sons (who attended Solihull School) and two daughters. Nicknamed Katie at school because of his initials, he was always called Terence[63]. Muriel was one of nine children of builder Bragg, as opposed to baker Bragg and butcher Bragg of Solihull (originally three brothers who went into separate trades. Thomas Bragg, the undertaker, was their first cousin)[64]. Dr Waters had originally been the company doctor at Fisher & Ludlow, but decided to set up his own practice. He held his surgery in the dining room of the house, and the contemporary Ordnance Survey map marks No 10 appropriately. One can still see where his plate was fixed on the front wall. In 1957-58 Edward & Eleanor Brooker were part of the household, but they had been replaced in 1959 by Reginald & Mary Woodham. The Waters marriage broke up and Terence went to live at 54 Bunbury Road, Northfield. He died tragically, aged only 50, on 21 September 1966. Probate for his estate, £10,684, was granted to his sons John Terence Waters, vetinerary surgeon, and Christopher James Waters, solicitor's articled clerk. Muriel moved with her children to 2 Witley Avenue, Solihull; she now lives in Guardian Court, New Road.

Ralph J. and Pamela ROBBINS were in residence from 1964 until 1972 with Julian,

[58] *GRO Index for Q/E June 1906 [Kings Norton 6c 963]*

[59] *GRO Index for Q/E March 1907 [Solihull 6d 616]*

[60] *GRO Index for Q/E December 1909 [Solihull 6d 598]*

[61] *GRO Index for Q/E June 1912 [Kings Norton 6c 702]*

[62] *Information from Mrs Muriel Waters (nee Bragg)*

[63] *Information from Mrs Muriel Waters (nee Bragg)*

[64] *Information from Miss Kathleen Saunders*

Nicola and Steven. By 1973 Peter L. and Barbara GRIFFITHS lived in the house, with their children Laura & Stephen. The latter left home in 1975 but Mr and Mrs Griffiths remained until 1981. The next occupants were Ronald & Gillian RAM, with Doris RAM, but they did not stay long as David and Denise BADDELEY had arrived by 1984. The Baddeleys remain in residence.

### No 12   NEWSTEAD / GREYSTONE

This large, two storey house shares some of the features found opposite at Nos 7 & 9 and 11 & 13, and probably all were designed by E.H.Wigley. Amongst the similarities noted by the Solihull Borough Conservation Architect in 1985 were *the types of windows, the cornice mouldings over the windows, the fireplace windows and the timber moulding used as the stop between brickwork & render. The single storey, central entrance is again a feature found across the road.*

As only 6 months had elapsed since he bought the land in March, this was probably the first plot that Joseph Albert Wells sold. The purchaser, on 17 October 1903 for £273-14s, was Albert Victor MARTINDALE, gentleman, of *Vellore,* The Driffold, Sutton Coldfield. The plot had a frontage of 24 yards *'in a new road called, or about to be called, Ashleigh Road'*; the depth was 80yds 1ft 6ins, making 1932 sq yds in area. The purchaser was subject to a 'proper proportion' of the cost of the maintenance & repair of Ashleigh Road *'until the same shall have been taken over by the District Council.'* Mr Martindale also had to erect a fence not less than 5ft, nor more than 7ft, high on the south & west boundaries. The building line was 10yds back from Ashleigh Road.

Albert Martindale had been born in 1864 in Handsworth, the son of Ralph Martindale, an edge tool manufacturer[65]. Described as an insurance office clerk, Albert was shown in the 1881 Census at home at 119 Birchfield Road, Handsworth with his widowed mother Emma (48) and his three brothers and three sisters. The family came originally from Yorkshire - his mother from Halifax and his eldest brother was born at Malton. From Victoria Road, Acocks Green, and now described as the Secretary to an insurance company, Albert married Helen Jones, a year older than himself, on 20 October 1891 at Holy Trinity, Birchfield. She was the daughter of Richard Jones, a manufacturing jeweller of 33 Trinity Road, Birchfield. Albert & Helen called their new house *Newstead*: it was one of the first to be erected in the road, and they lived in it until 1919. On 23 May 1906 Mr MARTINDALE mortgaged the property for £800 to H.A.Humphrey of 38 Victoria Street, Westminster. The interest rate was 4%. The mortgage was redeemed on 17 May 1915. When they left Ashleigh Road the Martindales moved to *The Oaks*, Hampton Lane. Albert, who had been described as an insurance manager when he sold *Newstead,* died aged 69 on 16 June 1933 worth £31,643-7-11d.

George Charles DEAN, tailor of 94 High Street, Birmingham, bought the property on 31 May 1919 for £2,000. He and his wife Ellen[66] renamed the house *Greystone.* They stayed only three years, and were perhaps attracted to leave by the profit they made on selling.

(Thomas) Alfred TUSTAIN, certified accountant of 39 Court Oak Road, Harborne,

---

[65] *Marriage Certificate*
[66] *Electoral Roll 1920*

bought *Greystone* on 11 September 1922 for £3,000. He lived in the house with his wife Edith Elizabeth (nee Pilsbury), daughter Edith Mary who had been born in 1907[67] and was listed in the 1929 electoral roll; and son John Pilsbury born in 1913[68] and shown on the 1934 roll. The 1930 electoral roll showed they had a servant named Emma Jane Bruce, but she was replaced by Alice Key in 1934. Alfred Tustain had installed a telephone, Solihull 207, by 1924 - one of only nine in the road at that time[69]. With the introduction of four figure numbers in 1931, it became Solihull 0207. Daughter Edith married (Alfred) Cecil Constantine of No 11 in 1931[70].

Mrs Tustain, described simply as of *Greystone,* Solihull, died aged 57 on 2 October 1934. Probate was granted to her husband, described as a tea company director, and her son, now a university student. Her estate amounted to £3,823-7-5d. Alfred then married Alice M.Ward in 1935[71]. The second Mrs Tustain was devoted to her pair of Siamese cats[72]. The Tustains moved to 76 St Bernards Road, Olton and the 1936 Kelly's Directory showed *Greystone* as empty. Mr Tustain retained ownership of the house until his death aged 69 on 20 January 1946. Probate for his estate (£267,770-18-5d) was granted to his son and Barclays Bank. In 1937 the house was let to Arthur & Daisy Louisa SMITH, with Frances Ford. Their telephone number was Solihull 0199.

On 17 August 1938 William Wooler WHARAM, insurance manager of 216 Orphanage Road, Erdington, signed a lease to rent *Greystone* for £110 a year, payable monthly in advance. He was obliged to keep the inside, including *'drains and sanitary & water apparatus'*, properly painted and in complete repair without any alteration; to permit the lessor to inspect the interior twice a year; not to use the premises other than as a private dwellinghouse; and not to sublet. The lessor had to keep the outside of the premises *'in tenantable repair'*. The lease was renewed, at the same rent, in 1942.

Mr Wharam bought *Greystone* on 28 May 1958 for £5,500 from Mr Tustain's executors (who included his son John Pilsbury Tustain of 109 St Bernards Road, Olton). The same day he raised a mortgage for the complete amount from The National Employers Mutual General Insurance Association Ltd. The interest rate was 4.5%. The mortgage was redeemed on 15 August 1973.

William Wharam, known as Billy, lived in the house with his wife Edna and daughter Jean Margaret. Arthur Porritt, Edna's father, lived with the family in his last years but died, aged 74, in 1947[73]. Their telephone number was Solihull 0199. Edna was a great gardener, besides being a gifted pianist & dressmaker[74]. Born in 1937[75], Jean became a physiotherapist who worked with Miss Stubbs at her premises on the corner of Solihull High Street and The

---

[67] *GRO Index for Q/E June 1907 [Kings Norton 6c 527]*

[68] *GRO Index for Q/E June 1913 [Kings Norton 6d 170]*

[69] *Kelly's Directory for Warwickshire 1924*

[70] *GRO Index for Q/E December 1931 [Solihull 6d 1678]*

[71] *GRO Index for Q/E December 1935 [Solihull 6d 1985]*

[72] *Information from Mrs Sheila Atterton*

[73] *GRO Index for Q/E March 1947 [Surrey Mid E.5g 554]*

[74] *Information from Mrs Muriel Waters (nee Bragg)*

[75] *GRO Index for Q/E March 1937 [Sutton Coldfield 6d 862]*

Square[76]. Later Jean received patients in the dining room at No 12[77]. She married Paul John Cartwright of Brueton Avenue in 1962[78], but he was killed in a motorway accident. She then became Mrs Abbey and lives at Alvaston. The better known Margaret Wharam - music mistress at St Martins School, organist & choirmistress of Solihull Methodist Church 1953-1993, and founder of the Margaret Wharam Choir in 1967 - was no relation. William died on 23 January 1963 aged 62 at The General Hospital, Birmingham. Probate for his estate (£9,374-14-1d) was granted to Barclays Bank. His widow, Edna, formally took ownership of the house on 24 September 1963 and continued to live there for another 10 years, when she moved to be near her daughter at Shottery. Edna, who had been born in Leeds on 31 March 1902, died on 26 December 1989 at Tutnall Hall Nursing Home, Tardebigge, near Bromsgrove. Her estate was less than £100,000.

On 15 August 1973 David Lee MILNE, a chartered accountant & company director, and Pamela Eva MILNE, his wife, both of 431 Cockfosters Road, Hadley Wood, Barnet, bought the property for £37,000. They came with their children Alexander (born 22 October 1962) & Kate. The telephone number changed to 705 0371. David became Finance Director of Glynwed and they moved to Lapworth in April 1980.

They were succeeded by Malcolm & Janet GARDNER with their son Michael (born 5 January 1969), who moved from No 31 Ashleigh Road. The present owners are Kevin & Jean DAVIS who arrived with Luke & Katie in 1986, and have since had five other children. They kindly lent their property deeds to provide the basis of the above information.

## No 14   THE OAKLANDS

The site for No 14, with a long frontage of 42 yards, was sold by Joseph Albert Wells of 78 Newtown Row, Birmingham to James Philip Pound DUTFIELD of Tennyson Road, Small Heath for £500. The Conveyance was dated 2 October 1905 and named the neighbour to the north (ie No 12) as Mr A.V.Martindale; to the south (ie No 20, since the land for Nos 16 & 18 had not yet been sold off) as Mrs A.Stokes; and to the west as Richard S. Chattock. James Dutfield was a coal merchant, but he was also the Secretary of The Birmingham Citizens Permanent Building Society and he took out a mortgage of £1,400 with which to build on the land.

Ernest H. Wigley, architect & surveyor of 121 Colmore Row, Birmingham designed the house in 1905 (we have a copy of the original plans), and formally notified the Rural District Council of the intention to build on 20 October. Approval was given by A.E Currall, the Surveyor on the 24th. Simon Herrick, the Solihull Borough Conservation Architect in 1985 wrote :

'*The front rates with No 19 as one of the two most dramatic in the street with its fine display of timber framing, tile hanging and the daring jetty at second floor level on the front gable. Under the jetty and within the tile hanging is an oriel window and below that the bay window to the Drawing Room. The house was originally designed with a coach house and a tackle & hay loft above. This is now the garage and its gable is timbered to match the house.*

---

[76] *Information from Mr David Patterson*
[77] *Information from Mrs Pam Johnson (nee Fox)*
[78] *GRO Index for Q/E December 1962 [Solihull 9c 1841]*

*No 14. Original elevation drawing signed by E.H.Wigley in 1905.*

*One or two differences between the drawings and the way the front elevation was actually built are apparent. The Drawing Room bay window was planned to be much larger whilst the Kitchen window (to the right of the central porch) has changed in proportion, the sill having been raised. The dormer window was given a small pediment which is not shown on the drawing. Wigley provided a Drawing Room, Dining Room, Kitchen, Hall, Lavatory, Larder, Scullery, Staircase Hall and a China Pantry. Nothing unusual about any of this except that the China Pantry is about as far away from the kitchen as it possibly could be.*

*On the first floor there are four large bedrooms and a bathroom. Bedroom No 1 (with the oriel window) has its own dressing room. On the second floor there are two further bedrooms and a huge billiard room. Billiard tables are extremely heavy items and here therefore the partition walls below are load bearing whilst the floor joists are increased in depth to support one and a half tons of Welsh slate.*

The garage was extended (probably before World War II) into the rear yard, which was covered with a glazed roof. A number of major internal alterations were made to the ground floor of the house by Mr & Mrs BROWN in the 1960s[79]. The larder, scullery, kitchen & tool room were all combined into one large through kitchen, and the fireplaces removed. Fireplaces were also removed from the bedrooms, although the chimneys were left in position.

James DUTFIELD had been born in 1858, the eldest son of James & Ann Dutfield. He was described in the 1881 Census as a wages clerk at the gas works, living with his family in Aston. He married Mary Cope on 28 April 1884 in Worcester, when he described himself as a coal merchant. This was the occupation he pursued for the rest of his life, and how he

---

[79] *Information from Mrs Pam Johnson (nee Fox)*

*Rear of No 14 about 1912. Compare with the next photograph.*

was described when buying the plot in Ashleigh Road. He & Mary had a son, Sydney born in 1885, and three daughters, Lillian, Amy & Dora born between 1887 and 1893. Sadly Mary died on 15 February 1899 after only 15 years of marriage. James then married Constance Aldridge, his cook-housekeeper, on 18 January 1900 at Salford Priors, Warwickshire. They appeared, with James' children from his first marriage, in the 1901 Census living at 40 Charles Road, Bordesley. They moved into the newly built house in Ashleigh Road as soon as it was finished in 1906, and stayed until 1916.

James was a prominent Freemason and was also active, together with Joseph Chamberlain, in the formation of the Liberal Unionist Party. He died in 1943. The Birmingham Post of Tuesday 21 December carried the following notice: *DUTFIELD. On December 18, James Philip Pound Dutfield, dearly beloved husband of Constance Lizzie, passed away at his residence Wood Lawn, Balsall Common near Coventry, aged 85 years. Manager & Secretary of Birmingham Citizens Permanent Building Society. Cremation Perry Barr Wednesday 22nd at 11am'.* Constance died, aged 89, in 1958. Further details of the Dutfield family are in Appendix II.

James Dutfield was the first resident in Ashleigh Road, and amongst the first in the village, to have a telephone installed in his house. The Birmingham & District Telephone Directory for 1908 gave the number as Solihull 15.

*Rear of No 14 in March 2002 showing changes to the kitchen and garage and to the upper sitting-room windows.*

James Charles COX, metal refiner of Wake Green Road, Moseley, bought the house on its plot of land measuring 64ft (frontage) & 241ft (depth) for £1,500 in a conveyance dated 20 July 1916. The house's telephone number was changed to Solihull 114. Born in 1869, James was the second of four sons of Thomas and Marion Cox who in 1901 lived at *The Dingle,* Bills Lane, Shirley. He had married Edith Mary Herbert in 1893[80] and they had a son, Stephen, who was born on 1 October 1899 in Knowle[81] He appeared on the 1922 electoral roll, and became a metal refiner like his father. Mr COX sold the property on 24 June 1922 for £2,600 and moved to *Woodbastwick,* Lode Lane where he died on 22 February 1925. Probate for his estate (£5,965-11-5d) was granted to his widow and son.

The purchaser was Eva DUGGAN, the wife of Thomas Foster DUGGAN, solicitor of Cannon Street, Birmingham. Thomas Duggan had been born in 1874[82] and had married his wife in 1902[83]. The couple lived in the house for nearly 14 years with their son Clement,

---

[80] *GRO Index for Q/E March 1893 [Solihull 6d 545]*
[81] *Birth Certificate*
[82] *GRO Index for Q/E December 1874 [Birmingham 6d 66]*
[83] *GRO Index for Q/E September 1902 [Birmingham 6d 247]*

*James Dutfield (1858-1943) and his son Sydney, (1885-1951) who lived at No.14 1906-1916, the period in which this photograph was probably taken.*

born in 1903[84], and daughters Norah, born in 1909[85], and Eva known in the family as Peggy. Norah married Henry Alan Gould in 1933[86] and Peggy married William Lees Price in 1936[87]. The telephone number continued to be Solihull 114 until 1931 when, with the introduction of four figure numbering, it became 0114. Although the house had been called *The Oaklands* since it was constructed, the 1935 telephone directory was the first to enter the name, previous residents being described simply as of Ashleigh Road. Between 1929 & 1934 the Duggans had a servant, Myra Gwendoline Nock, who was succeeded in 1935 by Rhoder Insell. On 16 January 1936 Mrs Duggan sold the property for £1,750, a considerable drop on the price she had paid, presumably indicating the difficult economic conditions of the time. The Duggans moved to *Broad Meadow,* Tiddington Road, Stratford-on-Avon. Thomas died aged 81 on 6 October 1955 worth £30,404-3-4d, his widow being his executor. After his death Eva moved along Tiddington Road to *White Holme* where she died on 18 March 1960. The executors of her estate (£81,901-7-2d) were her two daughters.

Charles HARDAKER of Newspaper House, Birmingham occupied the house for 12 years from 1936. He had been appointed Director & General Manager of The Birmingham

[84] *GRO Index for Q/E December 1903 [West Bromwich 6b 860]*
[85] *GRO Index for Q/E September 1909 [Kings Norton 6c 435]*
[86] *GRO Index for Q/E June 1933 [Meriden 6d 1318]*
[87] *GRO Index for Q/E September 1936 [Stratford 6d 2906]*

Gazette in 1933, having started his career as a journalist on The Northern Echo in Darlington (his birthplace) in 1902, and then moved to The Westminster Gazette in 1921[88]. He married Margaret on 29 June 1907 and they had three sons & a daughter. Charles died on 11 November 1948 at the Queen Elizabeth Hospital, Edgbaston, the administration of his estate (£22,079-18-6d) being granted to his widow. She continued to live in *The Oaklands*, of which she became the legal owner in July 1949, with their daughter Margaret, until 1951. The telephone number was Solihull 1472. She sold it on 30 May that year for £6,000.

Ernest George EVANS, golf ball manufacturer of 295 Warwick Road, Solihull, was the buyer and stayed for 8 years. The telephone number became Solihull 4446. He had married Ethel Beryl Edwards on 16 September 1933 at Christ Church. Sparkbrook[89]. Then aged 29, he was the son of William James Evans, a builder, of 1453 Stratford Road, Birmingham. She was a clerk aged 23, the daughter of William David Edwards, a boilermaker, of 156 Anderton Road, Sparkbrook. Ethel preferred to spell her first name Ethyl. They had a son David, born in 1939[90]. Ernest Evans sold the house for the same price as he had paid, to another local family on 1 December 1959.

John Moore BROWN of 32 Dorchester Road, Solihull, lived in the house with his wife, Lois, two sons & a daughter from 1959 to 1970. They were all asthmatics[91]. His father was principal of Hopwood & Gilbert, grocery wholesalers (with a warehouse near the Birmingham General Hospital) who lived in St Bernards Road, Olton, next to the parents of Dr Waters[92], who resided at No 10 Ashleigh Road from 1947 to 1962. John & Lois Brown made major alterations to the kitchen, and maintained a 'show' garden[93]. From their arrival the telephone number became 4188 and has remained so ever since. The BROWNs moved to Truro to set up a supermarket[94].

John Kaye and Elizabeth D.J.A.ROLLIT of 7 The Royal Hoylake, Wirral bought the house jointly on 16 July 1970 for £14,950. They had three sons (Richard, Edward & Jonathan, whose heights as they grew up are still recorded on the cellar door), and also a dalmatian dog to whom the garden was sacrificed. The Rollits stayed for seven years, during which property prices rose sharply. They sold it for £42,000 in 1977 and moved to Berkhamstead.

Nigel Ian and Angela Margaret CAMERON moved from 17 Daylesford Avenue, London SW15 on 18 August 1977. Nigel Ian worked for The Post Office and had been appointed Chairman of the Midlands Postal Board. Angela was a teacher who, soon after arriving in Solihull, was appointed a magistrate. They have three sons all educated at Solihull School - Peter (born 25 May 1966, a Royal Marine officer), Alastair (born 2 August 1967, a chartered accountant) and Colin (born 13 February 1970, a wine merchant). All are now married.

---

[88] *Birmingham Year Book*

[89] *Marriage Certificate*

[90] *GRO Index for Q/E March 1939 [Sutton Coldfield 6d 960]*

[91] *Information from Mrs Muriel Waters (nee Bragg)*

[92] *Information from Mrs Pam Johnson (nee Fox)*

[93] *Information from Mrs Olive Lacey*

[94] *Information from Mrs Pam Johnson (nee Fox)*

No 14 hosted two events in 1986 in connection with the designation of Ashleigh Road as a Conservation Area. On Friday 31 January Simon Herrick gave a lecture in the billiard room, and the original drawings of many of the houses were put on display. On Saturday 21 June he led a visit by the Victorian Society and they were entertained to tea in an appropriate style on the lawns. On Saturday 1 June 2002 the garden was the venue for the Ashleigh Road Queen's Golden Jubilee lunch party, to which 80 people came – aged from one to 97.

## No 16   GLENMIRE

In 1906 James DUTFIELD had a pair of semi-detached houses (also designed by Mr Wigley) built on the southern part of his site, so that the frontage of No 14 was halved to 21 yards. The new houses were named *Glenmire* and *Glenties,* and are now Nos 16 & 18 respectively. James retained ownership of these houses until 1918, ie 2 years after he had sold No 14.

*Glenmire*  was initially occupied by Alfred Dawson ZAIR[95]. Born in 1868[96], the 1881 Census recorded him, aged 13, as one of 44 boarders at Greenhill School, School Road, Kings Norton. His wife was Edith Harcourt and they had a son, Alfred Harcourt, born in 1907[97]. The family had moved out of *Glenmire* by 1916. Mr Zair died at *Lismoyne*, Lydford, Devon on 14 May 1923 and probate for his estate of £19,029-5-4d was granted to Edith Harcourt Zair, his widow, and John Weller Braithwaite, bank manager. The latter lived in Streetsbrook Road. Mrs Zair must have liked Solihull because on 5 November 1923 she bought No 3 Ashleigh Road (which she renamed *Lismoyne*) and lived there until she died in 1954.

The second tenant of No 16 was Thornton F.PITT[98]. The house was sold in December 1918 by James Dutfield to Hugh Lancelot ALDIS, manufacturer, for £1,150[99]. Hugh ALDIS was a member of a noted family of mathematicians, which included five high Wranglers (see Appendix III). He had been born on 26 August 1870 in Calcutta, the son of James Aldis, and was recorded with his family in the 1881 Census at 53 Lichfield Street, Walsall. Hugh was educated at the City of London School (1883-89) and Trinity College Cambridge (1889-92) where he graduated as 14th Wrangler. In 1893 he joined the staff of Messrs J.H.Dallmeyer Ltd, photographic lens & optical instrument makers in London. In 1900, with his brother Arthur, he founded Aldis Brothers of Sparkhill. The firm designed the Aldis lens for hand cameras and for projectors. During The Great War it produced the Aldis Lamp for signalling at sea; telescopic rifle sights, and the Aldis Unit sight for use on aeroplanes[100].

Hugh Aldis lived at *Glenmire*  from 1919 until 1938 but he never installed a telephone. His wife was Violet Ethel and they had two sons, Ralph Lancelot born in 1910[101], and Hugh Gabriel. Violet was not listed in the electoral roll after 1932. Her husband had already had two family deaths that year. His unmarried sister, Ethel Mary, who lived with his parents at

---

[95] *Kelly's Directory for Warwickshire 1908 & 1912*
[96] *GRO Index for Q/E March 1868 [Aston 6d 238]*
[97] *GRO Index for Q/E June 1907 [Solihull 6d 640]*
[98] *Electoral Roll 1916*
[99] *Information from Mr Ken Hewitt*
[100] *Alumni Cantabrigensis 1752-1900 by J.A.Venn, CUP 1940*
[101] *GRO Index for Q/E December 1910 [Solihull 6d 572]*

Minsmere, Dunwich (now the famous bird reserve) died on 8 February, and his mother Frances Emily died on 30 August. Hugh was the executor for each (estates worth £803 & £750 respectively). Hugh much enjoyed running his O gauge trains, whose track was laid out in the box room. Almost certainly at this time there was a maid, Betty Holden, who wrote her name and job title on the undecorated wall of the front bedroom at the top of the house[102].

In 1933 Ralph was listed on the electoral register, and his brother followed in 1934. Both had left home before 1937, which was the last year in which the electoral roll listed Hugh, the father. He went to live in *The Red House*, Sidmouth Road, Lyme Regis where he died on 18 July 1945. His estate was valued at £9,436-2-4d, and probate was granted at Llandudno to Lloyds Bank.

Maurice Angus and Dorothy Edith BARNES of 50 Silhill Hall Road bought *Glenmire* for £750 in April 1938[103]. Their telephone number was Solihull 0619 and they stayed for 10 years. They had married in 1929[104]. From at least 1945 until 1948 they had Eveline J.Hubbard living with them, who was Dorothy's mother.

In November 1948 the house was sold to Bryce Graham DEWSBURY, commercial manager of 28 Boden Road, Hall Green for £4000. The telephone number became Solihull 3221. Bryce lived in the house with his wife Elsie Florence (nee Searle), whom he had married in 1936[105], until September 1953. They sold it to Norman MARSTON, company accountant of Gladstone Road, Dorridge for £3100. His wife was Mary Josephine, and Amy Nellie Freeman lived with them[106].

Royston Richard LACEY of 18 Orchard Avenue, Solihull bought the property for £3150 in November 1955. The telephone number became Solihull 4495, which it remains today. Having worked for Cadbury's, Royston became an antique dealer with a shop called Harcourt Lacey on the corner of Poplar Road & Warwick Road, which was later taken over by Clive Silvester of No 13 Ashleigh Road. A year after Royston bought the house, planning permission was given to convert the cellar into a garage which required excavation of the entrance, and in 1972 he became the joint owner with his wife, Olive May. Olive, besides being a talented curtain maker, was such an expert cake decorator that her employers stipulated, when she retired, that she should not continue to do this.

Royston & Olive had five children, Mark, Aidan, Fergusson, Alison & Naomi. Mark married Carol but he was killed in an accident. They had Andrew & Rowland[107]. Aidan married Carol as her second husband in 1972[108]. Mrs Lacey decorated their wedding cake which included superb cameos of the two boys[109]. Aidan is a preacher at The Gospel Hall, Solihull, and travels abroad in this profession. He & Carol, using the surname

[102] *Information from Mr Ken Hewill*

[103] *Information from Mr Ken Hewitt*

[104] *GRO Index for Q/E December 1929 [Birmingham S 6d 151]*

[105] *GRO Index for Q/E June 1936 [Edmonton 3a 2213]*

[106] *Electoral Roll 1954*

[107] *Electoral Roll 1990*

[108] *GRO Index for Q/E December 1972 [Ploughley 6B 2535]*

[109] *Information from Mrs Sue Hewitt*

Harcourt-Lacey, live at 26 Fircroft, Solihull, with their daughter Pamela Ruth, born in 1975[110]. Fergusson became an off-shore financier. Alison died in a fire in Northern Ireland. Naomi (born 18 July 1955) joined the police force. After Royston's death Olive continued to live at No 16 until 1979 when she moved to Belfast to be near Alison.

The new owners were Ken & Sue HEWITT who moved from Backwell near Bristol to set up and run the UK marketing company of a Norwegian metals producer. They came with Philip (born 24 March 1966), (Alastair) John (born 10 September 1967) and Penny (born 7 August 1970). Ken retired in 1995.

### No 18   GLENTIES / RUAN

The first occupant was Alfred Wallace TREVITT[111]. He had been recorded in the 1881 Census as an 11 year old scholar living at home - 81 Spencer Street, Birmingham - with his parents, Enoch J.Trevitt (42), a master jeweller employing 4 men & 3 boys, and Catherine Trevitt (42). Alfred had two brothers and two sisters. The family had spent some years in The United States since Alfred and two younger siblings were born there. Alfred joined the family business and in due course succeeded his father. He visited South Africa to obtain diamonds, but not entirely successfully.

Alfred, then described as a commercial traveller of Heathfield Road, Birchfield, married Edith Louise Wood on 13 December 1898 at Holy Trinity, Birchfield[112]. She was six years younger than him, the daughter of George Wood, a farmer of Ashbourne. They had four daughters and two sons. The eldest, Marie Louise, born in November 1900, remained a spinster. She worked for a solicitor all her life and, after her mother's death in 1954, lived with her sister Irene at 15 Ralph Road, Shirley. She died on 13 September 1972. Irene Kathleen, born in November 1901[113], also stayed single. She remained at home with her parents and then moved with her sister Marie to Ralph Road, where she died on 23 January 1973. Rita Laughton was born on 16 March 1905, married Leslie Harold Sanders (1903-1988) in 1929[114], and died on 23 October 1995. Their son, Graham, became a priest and is now retired. Maureen Yardley, their daughter, has kindly supplied much of the information on the Trevitt family. Frank Laughton arrived in 1907[115], the first child to be born at No 18. Sadly he died on 2 November 1908 aged only 13 months and his small headstone is just outside the west door of St Alphege Church. Kittie Laughton was born in 1909[116], married Cyril F.Harrison in 1940[117] and died in 2001. (Alfred) Laughton was born in 1911[118], married Mildred Moody in 1938[119], and they had two sons - John and

[110] *GRO Index for Q/E September 1975 [Solihull 34 0658]*
[111] *Kelly's Directory for Warwickshire 1908 & 1912*
[112] *Marriage Certificate*
[113] *GRO Index for Q/E December 1901 [West Bromwich 6b 801]*
[114] *GRO Index for Q/E September 1929 [Solihull 6d 2286]*
[115] *GRO Index for Q/E December 1907 [Solihull 6d 617]*
[116] *GRO Index for Q/E June 1909 [Solihull 6d 659]*
[117] *GRO Index for September 1940 [Solihull 6d 3401]*
[118] *GRO Index for Q/E December 1911 [Solihull 6d 1224]*
[119] *GRO Index for Q/E June 1938 [Birmingham 6d 742]*

*No 18 in 1906.*
*Note the gate and walls.*

Christopher. Laughton died, aged only 52, in 1964[120]

The Trevitts were still the tenants when the house was sold in June 1918 by James Dutfield to Martha Elizabeth SMITH[121], but by 1920 they had moved to *Meriden* in Warwick Road. Later they moved to 8 Dorchester Road where Alfred died on 10 October 1945 leaving £293-19-11d. Edith died on 1 January 1954 worth £1,418-13-7d. Her two eldest (unmarried) daughters, who had lived with her, were her executors.

The 1920 electoral roll listed Martha Elizabeth SMITH, with her husband Frederick Philip, at *Glenties*. They had a son named Frank Thomas born in 1903[122], who appeared in the 1924 electoral roll. They were still there in early 1927, but the house seems to have been unoccupied in 1928 & 1929.

Ralph de Courcy DEYKIN and his sisters Eva Gertrude & Grace Helena DEYKIN were in residence by 1930 and changed the name of the house to *Ruan*. Ralph had been born on 26 October 1878 into a wealthy Edgbaston family. His father was William R.Deykin, a manufacturer of electroplate, who at the time of the 1881 Census was aged 47; his mother, Mary, was then 34. Ralph had four elder sisters, and the household at *Park Grange*, Somerset Road, was looked after by two housemaids and two nursery nurses. There was also

---

[120] *GRO Index for Q/E March 1964 [Surrey N. 5G 532]*
[121] *Information from Mr Ken Hewitt*
[122] *GRO Index for Q/E December 1903 [Worcester 6c 285]*

*Nos 18 and 16 in 1985 showing the entrances to the cellar garages made in 1956.*

a coachman. Ralph was educated at King Edward's School, Birmingham. A Director of Deykin & Harrison up to 1914, he served in The Great War and in 1915 was a Captain in the King's Liverpool Regiment. In 1928 he was appointed honorary secretary of the Birmingham Diocesan Board of Finance, and served until 1948. From 1935 he was also an elected member of the Church Assembly[123].

At No 18 Ralph and his sisters had a series of servants - Ada Nellie Redwood (1930-32), Ada Barker (1933-34) and Hilda L.Jones from 1935. Eva Deykin, spinster, died at sea aged 63 on 30 April 1938 leaving an estate of £11,073-6-7d, but Ralph and Grace were still living in the house in 1945, together with Hilda Jones. Mr Deykin did not have a telephone in 1935, but installed one (Solihull 2184) during the war. By 1946 the Deykins had left. In his last years Ralph lived at The Gold Hill Hotel, Malvern. He died in the Court House Nursing Home there, aged 87, on 17 December 1965 worth £42,651.

Eric & Monica EVANS lived in the house for a year before Francis W.M. WOODCRAFT and his wife Mabel arrived in 1947. They appear to have had the telephone removed (or went ex-directory). They had given way to Laurence Frederic & Clarice Muriel HANMAN by 1955, when the telephone directory again listed the number as Solihull 2184. Paul Humphreys, perhaps a lodger, lived with them[124]. Their daughter Patricia Martine became 21 in 1956, the year they left. David & Patsy LONG arrived from 7 Halford Road to live in the house, together with Lilian M. Barker. Assuming it was converted at about the

[123] *Birmingham Year Book 1939*
[124] *Electoral Roll 1955*

*Front elevation drawing of No 20 by De Lacy-Aherne, 1904. Note there are no plans for a garage.*

same time as No 16, the cellar became a garage with excavated entrance in 1956/57.

(Alfred James) Peter and Irene Dorothy THOMPSON came to No 18 before 1965 and stayed until 1983/84. They had David, Cheryl (b 3 March 1952), Andrea (21 June 1954) & Karen (20 October 1958), all of whom left home in various years between 1975 & 1982[125]. Their telephone number was Solihull 2359. Peter was in the motor trade. The Thompsons moved to Ludlow when they left, but later lived at *Little Orchard,* 36 Lower Montpelier Road, West Malvern, where Peter died aged 77 on 21 August 1999. Irene died in 2000 at the same age.

They were succeeded by Eric & Beverly WARD with their 5 children who left following their divorce in 1998. The house was then bought by Jeremy & Lisbeth PALSER who came with Joel (born 1995). Francesca was born to the house in 1998.

## No 20   THE COTTAGE / WESTFIELD / DINEDOR.

*'The architect was Mr H.De Lacy-Aherne of 5 Waterloo Street, Birmingham and his client was Mrs Stokes of Ascot Road, Moseley. Drawings were submitted to Solihull Rural District Council on 11 May 1904, and work would have started shortly after this date. The plans, elevations and sections are all carefully colour-washed and are extremely important because they pose considerable questions about the accepted 'Black & White' theme of Ashleigh Road.....The timber framing is shown dark brown, the infill panels are cream and*

---

[125] *Electoral Rolls*

the rest of the woodwork - windows, doors, porch, railings - is dark green; except the bargeboard which is pale green. Given that dark green was readily available at the time and very popular, the proposed colour scheme is hardly surprising. Black & white, green & buff, or any other colours could not change the fact that No 20 is a very attractive house. Elegant though his designs are, De Lacy-Aherne never really tackled the problem of designing a house for a corner plot. The house has only one 'front', whilst the equally important side to Silhill Hall Road has not been given any special consideration. Silhill Hall Road is shown (but not named) on the drawings and therefore it is clear that the Architect simply ignored the challenge.

The drawings show the usual range of ground floor accommodation with a generous entrance hall with its own fireplace. Upstairs the main bedroom ('Bedroom No 1') faces the back garden and is, by far, the largest. It has its own dressing room. One of the four bedrooms ( the smallest and facing No 18) is specifically designated 'Servants Bedroom'. The pitched roof garage is a later, but sympathetic, addition'. So wrote Simon Herrick, the Solihull Borough Conservation Architect in 1985.

Mrs Amelia STOKES of *Lyndale*, Ascot Road, Moseley in the county of Worcester was the wife of George Henry Stokes, jeweller. She bought the plot of land '*situate in and fronting to a new road called Ashleigh Road, leading from Warwick Road to Streetsbrook Road in the parish of Solihull, having a frontage of 26 yards and depth of 80 yards 1 foot 6ins*' from Joseph Albert Wells for £309-12s on 8 July 1904. The plot amounted to 2093 sq yards. The land to the west was the property of R.S.Chattock; to the north Joseph Wells; and to the south R.S.Chattock who had reserved it for a new road to be 14 yards wide. Mrs STOKES had to erect a fence not less than 5ft, or more than 7ft, within three calendar months on all sides of the land she was buying.

On 15 February 1905 Mrs Stokes, still with a Moseley address (indicating that her new house had not yet been completed), mortgaged her Ashleigh Road plot for £800 to Arthur William Woolley (electroplate manufacturer) of *Lapal Cottage*, Berkswell and Thomas Wallace Robinson (solicitor) of *Broxholme*, Wake Green Road, Moseley. The interest rate was 4%. The mortgage (for the same amount) was transferred on 21 October 1909 to A.W.Woolley (electroplate manufacturer, now of Kings Norton), Howard Frank Woolley (gentleman, of Bournmouth) and T.W.Robinson (solicitor, of Moseley). The Indenture mentioned that a dwellinghouse had now been built on the land. It is interesting to note that the same three mortgagees also lent £395 (at 4%) to Joseph Wells on 16 April 1913 against the security of No 3 Ashleigh Road.

The 1908 electoral roll, but not that of 1907, listed George Stokes of '*The Cottage*'. Mrs Stokes was not entitled to vote, despite owning the property. She had probably used her husband's money, since she was worth only £850-8-5d when she died aged 59 on 12 October 1922 at the Bevan nursing home, Sandgate (Kent). Her address was given as 10 Clifton Crescent, Folkestone. Her husband was still alive, although her executors were Ernest Thomas Woolley, electroplate manufacturer (possibly the son of one of the Woolleys who had provided her with a mortgage) & Dorothy Stokes, spinster.

Richard Edwin RILEY, jeweller, of 37 & 38 High Street, Birmingham bought *The Cottage* on 25 March 1914 for £945: he paid £145 to Mrs Stokes and £800 direct to the mortgagees (A.W.Woolley the electroplate manufacturer had now moved to Kingly,

*No 20 in 2002. Note the conservatory at the side.*

Alcester). The following day Mr Riley mortgaged the property with them for £500. The interest rate was still 4%. He redeemed this mortgage 18 months later, on 26 October 1915: Mr Woolley, the mortgagee, formerly the electroplate manufacturer living at Alcester, was now a Major in His Majesty's Forces with a Stechford domicile. Mr R.E. Riley, still of 37/38 High Street, Birmingham, sold the property on 29 March 1920 to Eric Richard Riley, manufacturer, of *Woodlyn*, Alderbrook Road, Solihull for £1,000. It is not known whether they were related. After only a year, and making £500 profit in the process, Mr Eric Riley sold the property, now called *Westfield*, although the conveyance still referred to him as of *Woodlyn*, Alderbrook Road. It would seem that neither of the Rileys ever lived in their Ashleigh Road property, but rented it out.

Their tenant from 1915 was John PARTRIDGE, a retired bank cashier, and his wife Caroline, who had rented No 11, naming it *Westfield*, from 1905. They brought that house name with them but not their children who, since they were no longer listed in the electoral roll, had presumably left home. In 1921 the Partridges moved to Devon, and lived at *Wayside*, 10 Oldway Road, Paignton. Caroline died on 2 May 1933 at *Holly Bank*, Primley Park, Paignton. The executor for her estate (£3,288-14-10d) was her daughter Gertrude, still a spinster. John moved within Paignton to 7 Southfield Avenue, where he died on 6 February 1942 aged 89 worth £11,657-17-10d. His executor was Lloyds Bank, presumably the bank for which he had worked during his life.

Henry Harold Aubrey TURNER, coal merchant of 38 Wills Street, Lozells, Birmingham bought *Westfield* from Eric Riley on 15 April 1921 for £1500. The son of George Turner, an engineer, Henry had been born in 1882[126]. He was described as a traveller when, aged 23, he married Gertrude in 1905[127]. She was two years older than Henry and was the daughter of the late John Leach, who had been a boilermaker. Henry and Gertrude lived in the house for 10 years. They never installed a telephone.

On 8 May 1931 Mrs Florence Victoria Mary ROBINSON (nee Rogers), the wife of Frederick John ROBINSON, works manager of 13 Richmond Park Road, Olton, bought the house for £1400. The same day she mortgaged the property for £800 to Lloyds Bank (interest rate not stated), which she redeemed on 11 March 1933. Soon after they arrived the Robinsons renamed the house *Dinedor* and installed a telephone (Solihull 0915), but do not appear to have had any living-in servants to begin with. From 1938 to 1940 Grace Hawksrigg was shown in the electoral roll, and in 1945 Sarah Gillis: presumably they were servants. The Robinsons had a daughter, Jean Elizabeth, born in 1925[128] who attended the Tree School in Warwick Road[129] and later appeared in the 1946-50 electoral rolls. She married Gerald B.Adams in 1953[130].

On 19 May 1951 Mrs Robinson, now of 126 Foxley Lane, Purley, Surrey sold *Westfield* for £5500 to Eric Charles TYLER of 5 Pinfold Road, Solihull. Two days later he mortgaged the property for £2000 to Beacon Insurance Co. The interest rate was 4%. The mortgage was redeemed on 24 August 1966. Eric & Sylvia Tyler retained the name *Dinedor* but their telephone number became Solihull 2148. Mr Tyler sold 695 sq yards of the rear garden, with a frontage of 80 foot to Silhill Hall Road, to Padrow (Birmingham) Ltd on 7 January 1964 for the construction of a bungalow, but no price is quoted in the papers. Eric Tyler was a Director of Tube Investments. With his wife Sylvia, and children Christopher & Ann, he continued to live in the house until 1966, when the family moved to Moreton-in-Marsh[131].

The purchaser on 25 August 1966 of the property, now quoted as having 1398 sq yards, was David Wallace GOSSAGE of 107a Metchley Lane, Harborne, Birmingham. He paid £10,250. His wife was called Margaret and they had a son, James (who became 18 on 4 April 1978). But the Gossages lived in the house only intermittently, as David worked abroad for Shell. The electoral rolls for 1970, 1974, 1975, 1976 and 1982 listed no occupants. The house was probably rented out, but the tenants did not register as voters. The house retained its telephone number (2148) and still carried the name *Dinedor* (on its garage door).

That name was removed when Richard & Judy INGRAM acquired the house on 27 September 1985. It was they who kindly provided the above information from Conveyances and Mortgage Indentures.

---

[126] *GRO Index for Q/E September 1882 [Thanet 2a 901]*
[127] *Electoral Roll 1922*
[128] *GRO Index for Q/E September 1925 [Solihull 6d 1311]*
[129] *Information from Mrs Diana Mitchell MBE*
[130] *GRO Index Q/E June 1953 [Coventry 9c 1492]*
[131] *Information from Mrs Muriel Waters (nee Bragg)*

# 6. HOUSES 22 TO 38

## No 22   LYNWOOD

Simon Herrick in 1985 considered that '*Nos 22 & 24 started life in about 1910 as a handed pair. Since then, No 22 has been carefully extended over the garage, and both have received minor alterations to their glazing bars but certainly nothing to detract from the general order and discipline. Each house is basically an L shape, with two storeys, hipped roof and front gable. They are rendered at first floor. The obvious care and attention that went into the first floor extension of No 22 is devalued not only by the existence of 112 Silhill Hall Road (*where No 22 used to have its tennis court) *but the way in which the latter's garage abuts No 22.*

The house dates in fact from 1905/6 since its first occupant - Stanley COOPER - appeared in the 1907 Electoral Roll, one of only 10 voters in Ashleigh Road. He remained in the house until at least 1916[1] but, since women did not gain the vote until 1918, it is not known whether he had a wife. Stanley had been born in 1874 at Henley-in-Arden, the second son of Robert and Sophia Cooper. The 1881 Census showed the family, which also included two daughters, in the High Street, Wootton Wawen. Robert was a land agent & valuer. Stanley was succeeded in 1920[2] by John Bristow Tucker, who named the house *Lynwood* but soon moved to *Whitecroft,* Birmingham Road. Nothing else is known about him except that he died on 12 December 1967 at 40 Pearce Avenue, Parkstone, Poole, worth £75,326.

Edwin James and Florence DEVIS arrived early in 1921[3]. Mr Devis had exactly the same names as his father who had been listed as a potato merchant aged 26 in the 1881 Census with his wife, Sarah Letitia, at 14 Heath Mill Lane, Aston. In the 1920s Mr & Mrs Devis senior lived at *Gowan Lea House* in Lode Lane. Edwin had been born in 1883[4], and married Florence Henrietta Seaman at All Saints, Bloxwich on 21 October 1908[5]. Aged 26, she was the daughter of George Seaman, gentleman, of 75 New Street, Birmingham. Edwin's sister Maud was one of the witnesses.

By 1929 Edwin & Florence had a servant, Esther Neate, who was still with them in 1937. George Seaman joined the household in 1931 and likewise was still there in 1937. A telephone (Solihull 620) was installed by May 1930 which, with the introduction of 4 figure numbering in 1931, became Solihull 0620. The house was empty in early 1938. When Mr Devis senior died aged 84 on 25 January 1940, Edwin was described as a wholesale fruit & potato merchant. He survived his father by only five years, dying on 27 November 1945 at

---

[1] *Kelly's Directory for Warwickshire1916*

[2] *Electoral Roll 1920*

[3] *Electoral Roll 1921*

[4] *GRO Index for Q/E June 1883 [Aston 6d 260]*

[5] *Marriage Certificate*

his home 16 Blythe Way. Probate for his estate of £20,875-15-1d was granted to his widow, who herself died aged 79 on 1 September 1960. Together they share a headstone in Robin Hood Cemetery with his father, mother (who died aged 72 on 13 July 1933), and sister Maud Eliza, who died unmarried aged 82 on 18 April 1963.

Harry and May BLOOMER, with their son (Harry) Clifford arrived in 1939[6]. Born in 1878, Harry was the fourth of six sons (all born in Halesowen) of Giles Thomas Bloomer, a wrought nail manufacturer, and his wife Ann. The 1881 Census showed the family living at *Park Field,* Lapal, Worcester with three servants. By 1901 they had moved to Warwick Road, Olton. Giles, at 62, had retired; Thomas (28), William (26) and Arthur (25) were all cabinet manufacturers; Edward (22) was a bankers' clerk; and the youngest, Frank, was not listed. Harry, then 23, was already an architect. He married May in 1906[7] and when they came to Ashleigh Road they had a servant, Mona Daffy. Their telephone number was Solihull 1915. Mrs Bloomer died aged 59 on 30 March 1941 worth £4,771-13-2d.

By 1945 Mary E. Whyatt had become the house servant. In 1946 she and Clifford had disappeared, and Harry had Roger and Margaret Harley with him; they remained until Harry's death on 25 March 1954. The executor for his estate (£48,503-11-3d) was his son. Clifford Bloomer had been born at Olton on 1 February 1909 and educated at Denstone College and the Birmingham School of Architecture. He qualified as an architect in 1933 and went into his father's practice, Harry Bloomer & Sons, Architects & Surveyors, 73 Hagley Road, Birmingham, dealing with banks, schools and commercial factory buildings. Clifford was consultant architect to the Birmingham War Factories Joint Committee 1940-45. Elevated to FRIBA, he was Vice-President of the Birmingham & Five Counties Architectural Association and Hon.Treasurer RIBA West Midlands. He was appointed MBE. He married Joan Edith Rycroft in 1952 and had a son: they lived at 24 Frederick Road, Edgbaston[8]. Clifford died on 23 September 1996 worth £760,587.

Reginald Stanley and Kathleen Mary EGERTON arrived in 1955. Reginald had been born on 1 April 1909, became a chartered accountant, and married Kathleen Bristow in 1938[9]. The telephone number of the house became Solihull 0467. The Egertons reduced the size of the garden by having No 108 Silhill Hall Road built[10] for Reginald's mother, Alice Jane Egerton, and his sister, Eva[11]. Alice died aged 82 on 8 May 1964, ironically at 22 Ashleigh Road[12], and probate for her estate (£26,317) was granted to Reginald, Dorothy Mary Tippetts, married woman, and Joseph Graham Egerton, local government officer. Eva, who had been born on 14 August 1907, continued to live alone in No 108 until 1990[13]; she died in 1993[14]. But Reginald and Kathleen stayed at No 22 only until about 1967 when they

---

[6] *Electoral Roll 1939*

[7] *GRO Index for Q/E December 1906 [Dudley 6c 82]*

[8] *Birmingham Year Book 1991*

[9] *GRO Index for Q/E September 1938 [Surrey NW 2a 1158]*

[10] *Information from Harry & Anne Lavery*

[11] *Electoral Roll 1962*

[12] *Probate Index of Wills*

[13] *Electoral Roll 1990*

[14] *GRO Index for 1993 [Birmingham 0611F 50A 064 0793]*

moved to *Fletchers,* Evenlode, Moreton-in-Marsh. Reginald died there on 14 November 1978 worth £32,710.

The house then had two different occupants in quick succession. Dennis & Betty KITCHING arrived with their son Charles, and Frederick Tocknell. They retained the 0467 telephone number, but were succeeded in early 1971 by John & Barbara CHAMBERS. They had two daughters. He was a builder/developer who reduced No 22's garden even further. On its Ashleigh Road corner he built No 112 Silhill Hall Road, into which he and his family moved in 1972[15] and where they stayed until 1977.

Harry and Anne LAVERY arrived in June 1972 with their 4 children (Judith born 12 March 1957, Christopher born 5 August 1958, Ailsa born 28 July 1960, and James born 11 November 1964). The telephone number changed to 705 5399. An Ulsterman from Belfast at whose university he had graduated, Harry had joined Unilever at Port Sunlight where he met his wife. They moved to Old Welwyn where Harry was involved in the company's food research & development. He was appointed Managing Director of Cadbury Typhoo, which brought the family to Solihull, and later became a director of Cadbury-Schweppes. Harry took part in the 1976 BBC Money Programme on Ashleigh Road. As a means of getting to know people, Ann collected for a major charity up and down Ashleigh Road, but found a number of the residents so rude that she switched to Broad Oaks Road who were much more friendly. A golfer, she was also active in the United Reformed Church. With their children away from home, the Laverys left No 22 in 1986 and moved to a smaller house in Pool Meadow Close

Loss-adjuster Mike NELSON-SMITH and his wife Sally-Jane, or SJ as she is known to her friends, arrived from Bromley (Kent) in June 1986 with daughter Francesca (born July 1985). Kirsty, born in January 1987, and Jinnie, born in July 1988, were born into the house.

## No 24   MARLBOROUGH

The first occupant was Charles THURSFIELD[16] who named the house *Marlborough*. It is one of only five houses in the road which still bears its original name, the others being Nos 14, 17, 28a and 29. Charles was recorded aged three months in the 1881 Census at 3 Back, 21 Long Acre, Aston with his father Thomas, a gun implement maker aged 38, and mother Emma (35), three sisters and two brothers. Charles left *Marlborough* in 1912.

The next occupant was Delavel STORY from Ulverley Green[17]. Aged 2, Delaval had been recorded in the 1881 Census at Lamerton, near Tavistock in Devon. His father, Edmund a merchant aged 45, and his mother Ellen (41) both came from Gateshead, and his two brothers and two sisters had all - like Delaval - been born at Byker in Northumberland. Besides a teacher and a nurse, the family had three domestic servants. Delaval was described as a secretary when on 22 May 1906 he married Mildred Eveline Wills at St Andrew, Plymouth[18]. She was the daughter of Thomas Greek Wills, a merchant of that city. In Ashleigh Road, Delaval & Mildred did not use the house name and had left by 1915. Their

---

[15] *Information from Harry & Anne Lavery*

[16] *Electoral Roll 1908*

[17] *Electoral Roll 1913*

[18] *Marriage Certificate*

final address was *Linden,* Harper Lane, Radlett. Delavel died on 14 August 1953 at St Albans City Hospital. Probate for his estate (£1,688-3-8d) was granted to Joan Primrose Story, spinster.

Arthur WARD was the next occupant[19]. Henry Norton SKERRETT had arrived by 1920[20]. He had been born on 3 January 1886 and married Ethel Agnes North on 25 July 1914 at St Saviour, Saltley[21]. She was 21 years old, the daughter of Edwin North, a railway inspector, of 22 Ellesmere Road, Saltley. Henry, 28, lived at 28 Wake Green Road, Moseley, and was a patent agent like his father, also called Henry. Henry and Ethel had William H. born in 1915[22] and Dorothy J. in 1919[23]. By 1924 they had a telephone, Solihull 116 (as one of only nine in the road), which with the introduction of 4 figure numbering in 1931 became Solihull 0116. The 1930 Electoral Roll listed two servants - Sarah Macbeth and Florence Powell - of which the latter was still with them in 1935. Towards the end of their lives the SKERRETTs moved to *Driftings,* Langley Road, Claverdon where Henry died on 9 May 1969 worth £20,207.

Herbert Griffiths CROSS became the owner of the house in 1935[24] and the telephone number changed to Solihull 1322. But he did not remain long, as the 1936 telephone directory listed him at *Dinedor,* Manor Road, Dorridge and the 1938 directory at 91 Silhill Hall Road. Towards the end of his life he moved to 3 Redcliffe Gardens, Leamington. He died on 22 April 1966 at Warwick Hospital. The executor for Herbert's estate (£864) was Philip Anthony Cross, who was an engineer and his son.

By 1937[25] the owners were Joseph W. and Annie KINCHIN. Joseph was the proprietor of the Solihull Motor Company in the High Street, above which they had lived[26] before coming to Ashleigh Road. Annie, nee Wichello, was the daughter of a Spanish family whose business at Camp Hill stables provided draught horses for haulage. They had married in 1913[27]. On their arrival at No 24, the telephone number became Solihull 0844. During the war they had a succession of American Army Officers, both male & female, billeted on them. When they left, Joseph & Annie moved to Yew Tree Farm, Chadwick End, where Joseph died on 23 December 1969 worth £12,656. Annie moved to 19 Beauchamp Avenue, Leamington, and died on 17 September 1971. They had three sons: Joseph born in 1914[28], Leslie 1915[29] and Victor 1917[30] who emigrated to South Africa in 1956[31]. Leslie, listed at

[19] *Kelly's Directory for Warwickshire 1916*
[20] *Electoral Roll 1920, but mistakenly listed his second name as Morton.*
[21] *Marriage Certificate*
[22] *GRO Index for Q/E September 1915 [Solihull 6d 1414]*
[23] *GRO Index for Q/E March 1919 [Solihull 6d 1085]*
[24] *Telephone Directory 1935*
[25] *Electoral Roll 1918*
[26] *Electoral Roll 1932*
[27] *GRO Index for Q/E March 1913 [Kings Norton 6d 73]*
[28] *GRO Index for Q/E March 1914 [Kings Norton 6d 33]*
[29] *GRO Index for Q/E June 1915 [Kings Norton 6d 24]*
[30] *GRO Index for Q/E March 1917 [Kings Norton 6d 30]*
[31] *Information from Mrs Beryl Kinchin*

home in 1937[32], served as an Intelligence Officer in the Far East during the Second World War. He married Beryl J.Lea in 1946[33]. They lived at 16 Broad Oaks Road and seem to have been connected with the Chadwick Hunter Stud at Chadwick End. Beryl, now widowed, lives today in Dorridge.

Oliver Eastman and Alice Ethel O'SHAUGHNESSY arrived in 1947. Oliver had been born on 14 April 1889 and married Alice Spinner in 1914[34]. After the war they had a daughter, Nora, born in 1920[35]. By 1948 they had a servant Rose Lowe, although the latter had left by 1955. Their telephone number remained as Solihull 0844. Alice died aged 77 on 20 June 1963: her husband, described as a company director, was the executor of her estate (£4,121-13s). He and Nora left the house in 1966 and went to live at 28 St Helens Road, where Oliver died on 15 August 1981 worth £28,114. Nora continued to live there until 1996.

There was then a series of occupants in quick succession. Alan & Ann LISLE, with Leslie Bates 1968-71; Edward & Leslye DUNKLEY with Michael & Julia, and Winifred Berry 1972-75 (when the telephone number was 3780); Brian & Myfanwy FISHER 1976-77; and Alan & Patricia CAMPBELL 1979-83 - by which time the telephone number had become 705 2548. The Campbells had a small son called Josh and, when they left Ashleigh Road, moved out to Eastcote[36]. Alan & Sally JAMES (nee Taylor) arrived in 1984, married in 1989, and are the current owners. Mark Taylor was also listed in 1990-94 and again in 1997, and James Taylor (born 28 May 1973) in 1991-96: they are Sally's sons from her first marriage.

## No 26  COTSWOLD

*Nos 26 & 28 are a handed pair of detached houses with semi-detached garages. They are predominantly brick, although their two storey bay windows have some applied timbering at first floor level. The gables of the houses and the garages all have a novel brick detail, which takes the form of three tall & very narrow niches, the middle one higher than the others[37].*

The house was bought in 1907 for £1,100[38] by Christopher COLLINS. He was listed in Kelly's 1908 Directory and was still there in 1916. His eponymous company at 30-32 St Paul's Square, Birmingham were shop lamp manufacturers. The 1881 Census had described him, aged 45 (born at Tewkesbury), as a Master Lamp Manufacturer employing 9 men, 3 boys & 3 girls. He was recorded at his home, 100 Gerard Street Aston, with his wife Mary Ann (also 45, born at Overbury, Glos.), her unmarried sister Louisa Booth (41), niece Kate Hammond (15, born at Tewkesbury) & Mary Ann Webb (21), domestic servant. They seem to have had no children. Mr Collins was described as a retired lamp manufacturer when he died on 6 October 1920. He was a rich man as his estate was valued at £39,221-1-3d. His widow Mary Ann continued to live in the house until her death, aged 91, on

---

[32] *Electoral Roll 1937*
[33] *GRO Index for Q/E September 1946 [Solihull 9c 2419]*
[34] *GRO Index for Q/E March 1914 [West Ham 4a 527]*
[35] *GRO Index for Q/E June 1920 [West Ham 4a 989]*
[36] *Information from Harry & Anne Lavery*
[37] *Ashleigh Road Conservation Area by Simon Herrick*
[38] *Information from Mr Michael Sansbury*

15 September 1927. Probate for her estate (£1,355-1-3d), other than settled land, was granted to William Burton, watch-case maker, and Bertha Turley, the wife of William Turley. The executors for her settled land (£1,700) were Herbert Norman, insurance agent, and Charles Albert Hayward, quantity surveyor. Gardner Tyndall, solicitor, was an executor of both estates.

Harry MARRABLE had moved in by 1928. Born in 1889[39], the 1929 Electoral Roll named him formally as Henry Howard MARRABLE and his wife as Ellen (nee Allen). They had married on 4 March 1911 at Brentford Register Office. Harry was 21 and described as a clerk living in Hanwell. Ellen was a year older, but both were already fatherless[40]. Harry and Ellen had three children. Marjorie Olive, born in 1913[41], appeared on the electoral roll 1936-39. Beatrice J. (but known as Bessie) was born in 1919[42], and Douglas H. in 1921[43]; the latter two were added to the roll in 1945. Douglas was at Solihull School with Peter FOX (see below), left home in 1946, became a development engineer, married and then divorced[44]. Bessie was shown with her parents on the Electoral Roll until 1948. The Marrables never installed a telephone. In 1946 Albert & Winifred Burrows had been part of the household. Harry Marrable died on 20 September 1948.

By July 1949 Hanbury DUNNETT had arrived and he immediately installed a telephone (Solihull 2536). The 1950 Electoral Roll listed the occupants as Hanbury Dunnett, Mary Regina Walker & Selina Florence De Souza; the last being replaced by David Hanbury Walker in 1955. The latter had left by 1960, leaving Hanbury Dunnett and Mary Walker still in residence.

In 1962 Peter and Patricia FOX came to live in the house, and the telephone number changed to Solihull 2421 (which it remains today). Peter was the brother of Pam Johnson who has lived at No 2 since 1961, and inherited the family knitting manufacturing business, called Arden Knitware, in Loveday Street, Birmingham. Despite using the most advanced Swiss machinery, it went bankrupt due to the high level of wages required to compete for labour with the car industry. Peter became a representative for another company in the same line of business and, with his wife, left No 26 in 1968 to live in the Cotswolds. They emigrated to Canada in 1975 and he died in 1999.[45]

In 1968 Thomas G. & Evelyn M. IRVINE moved into the house. They had a daughter Evelyn A. who was in the Forces (and shown as such in the Electoral Rolls from 1968-72). By 1973 Terence & Lois DILLON were in residence but they only stayed a short time. He was a teacher and left to be the headmaster of a comprehensive school in Nottingham[46].

Michael and Vera SANSBURY arrived in 1975 with their children Yvonne (who was 18 on 30 June 1985) & Paul (18 on 3 October 1986). They stayed until 1994 by which time

---

[39] *GRO Index for Q/E December 1889 [W Ham 4a 4]*
[40] *Marriage Certificate*
[41] *GRO Index for Q/E September 1913 [Uxbridge 3a 89]*
[42] *GRO Index for Q/E June 1919 [Solihull 6d 1093]*
[43] *GRO Index for Q/E June 1921 [Solihull 6d 1666]*
[44] *Information from Mrs Pam Johnson [nee Fox]*
[45] *Ibid*
[46] *Information from Mr Michael Sansbury*

*No 28 and the garage of No 26 in 2002, part of a handed pair built in 1907. Note the unusual detail of the gables and the wide Art Nouveau windows of the porch.*

their marriage had ended in divorce. Vera is remembered for regularly walking up Ashleigh Road with a parrot on her shoulder. She was a distant relation of the Russian Imperial family[47]: her great grandmother was a lady-in-waiting to the last Czarina. Michael taught languages at Solihull School for many years. Yvonne passed out top of her year at Birmingham Law School and then worked for Wragges before marrying and starting a family. Malcolm & Jane FLETCHER arrived in 1995 and are the current owners.

### No 28   ST MARY
This house was originally on a double plot and had a tennis court on its southern side[48]. This land was built on in 1954/5 when No 28a was erected.

Neville Smith HEELEY lived at *St Mary* in 1908[49] with his wife, Eliza Morgan. The 1881 Census had described him, aged 43 (born in Birmingham), as a Steel Toy Maker employing 41 men, 17 women & 2 boys. He was recorded at his home, 113 Soho Hill, Handsworth, with his wife (aged 37) and 3 children - Francis 15, Herbert 14 and Mary 12. The family had two servants. Apart from Francis, the family were still at the same address

---

[47] *Information from Harry & Anne Lavery*
[48] *Information from Mrs Pam Johnson (nee Fox)*
[49] *Kelly's Directory for Warwickshire 1908*

in 1891. Neville and Eliza lived at *St Mary* until Neville died on 26 March 1911 worth £17,739-11-6d. *The Birmingham Post* of Thursday 30 March contained the following item: *The funeral of Mr Neville Smith Heeley, Chairman of Directors of James Heeley & Sons, Hampton Street, took place yesterday. The first part of the ceremony took place at Solihull Wesleyan Church, the Rev'd S.Marriott officiating. The interment took place at Handsworth Old Church later in the day, the Rev'ds E.Heslem (Handsworth) & Marriott conducting the service.* Neville's widow continued to reside at *St Mary*[50].

By 1920 Herbert William Heeley, their second son and a bachelor, had joined his mother. In 1929 Nellie Elizabeth Martin & Laura Morgan Capner, probably servants, lived with them. In 1930 they had been replaced by Frances Geraldine Butler, who in turn was replaced by Dorothy Vines in 1931. The first mention of a telephone was in 1932[51] when the number was Solihull 0112. Herbert was fond of his alcohol and on one occasion was returning home with Williams, the driver of the local horse-drawn cab with whom he had been drinking, when the cab overturned on the corner of Ashleigh Road[52]. 'Cabbie Williams' had plied his trade at the station for many years, but his unhurried world was coming to an end. One evening he approached a traveller from the 'Businessman's Express': *'Cab Sir?' 'Not tonight, Williams, I'm in a hurry'.*

Eliza Heeley moved into a nursing home and died on 6 January 1937 aged 92. Probate for her estate (£1,221-16-11d) was granted to her sons, Francis Neville and Herbert William. The latter lived in the house only four more months before dying on 2 May 1937 at 40 Claremont Road, Handsworth, the home of his brother who was the executor of his estate (£14,486-14-10d).

In early 1938 the house was bought by Harry and (Annie) Ethel ASTBURY (nee Cartwright). For the first year only Florence Aldridge, presumably a servant, was with them. Mrs Astbury had previously been Mrs Wheelock[53] and her children by that marriage lived with them - Patricia in 1945 and 1946 and Michael John (who had been on the Services Register in 1946, giving this address) in 1947 to 1952. Harry & Ethel were by themselves from 1953 onwards. Their telephone number was Solihull 1013. By 1953 that part of the garden to the south of the house, which contained the tennis court, had been sold off for the building of No 28a. Harry died aged 78 on 12 January 1958. Probate for his estate (£51,174-1-4d) was granted to J.W.Smith (solicitor) and B.E.Bockington (certified accountant). In 1960 the Electoral Roll showed his widow sharing the house with Joseph & Margaret Dixon. William & Audrey Prince were with her in 1965; Judith Boutell & Denah Farrington in 1970; and Ellen Peters in 1973. In 1974 & 1975 Ethel Astbury was alone. She then moved into a flat and died a few years later.

Michael and Elizabeth BRADBURY arrived in 1976 with their children Mark and Susan (born 8 April 1963), and stayed for five years. Their telephone number was 704 9040. They were succeeded by (Ioan) Christopher and Margaret MORGAN[54], who continue to

---

[50] *Kelly's Directory for Warwickshire 1912 & 1916*
[51] *Kelly's Directory for Warwickshire 1932*
[52] *Information from Mr Bill Dewbury*
[53] *Ibid*
[54] *Electoral Roll 1982*

*No 28a in 2002, designed by Peter Hing in 1954.*

own the house today They have 6 children – Julian, Christopher, Georgina, Oliver (b 1978), Annabel & Edward. But the family were frequently in Malawi, where Chris works and where several of the children were educated, and so the house was let – for example to Martin & Hilary WILLIAMS in 1984/5 and Thomas & Gerda FIKKERT in 1989/90[55], or left empty. The current occupants are Michael & Susan ROSE.

### No 28a  ROSEGARTH
The house was designed in 1954 by Peter Hing who had designed No 38 in 1922. It was built at a cost of £5,400[56] on the former tennis court of No 28.

The 1957 electoral roll showed the first occupants as Norman & Joyce HURST. Florence Rooker was also listed by 1959, but had disappeared the following year. Arthur & Olga GODDARD had become the owners in 1962 and stayed for five years.

By 1968 Costas & Colette STELLAKIS had arrived with Dorothy Wyles. Louise STELLAKIS appeared on the electoral roll from 1978 to 1984, and Michael (born on 25 January 1967 who attended Solihull School) from 1984 to 1992. Dorothy Wyles died in 1992. Mr & Mrs Stellakis remain in residence.

---

[55] *Electoral Roll 1989 & 1990*
[56] *Ashleigh Road Conservation Area by Simon Herrick*

**No 30   SYLWOOD / MARSTON**

In 1985 Simon Herrick wrote *'No 30 is a rugged, chunky looking house of about 1905 with a hipped roof and a gabled front, set off-centre. It is predominantly of brickwork, with a small section of framing above the porch, to the left hand side. Within this timbered area is a flat roof dormer. The gabled front contains a two storey, six-sided bay window. The other example of the six-sided bay window occurs at No 1. More usually they have five sides or they are simply splayed. Over the bay there is an eliptical relieving arch which, as in Numbers 2 & 4, is both structural and decorative'.*

Joseph GLOSTER, the younger, of *The Croft*, Acocks Green, silversmith, bought the 1288 sq. yd. plot (16 yds frontage by 80 yds 1ft 6ins depth) from Joseph Albert Wells on 13 July 1909 for £225-8s. The land to the north had already been sold to Neville Heeley, but that to the south still remained in Joseph Wells' possession. Joseph Gloster senior lived at Streetsbrook House in Streetsbrook Road[57]. 'Our' Joseph took some time to have his new house built as he did not appear even in the 1911 Electoral Roll. Kelly's Directory of 1912 listed him, with the name of the house as *Sylwood*. His wife was Katie Florence nee Jackson, and they had two daughters. Barbara Joan was born on 22 September 1915 at *Sylwood*[58], and married Kenneth W.Grimsley in 1940[59]; and Kathleen B. born in 1917[60] who married Charles P.Clarke[61] three months before her elder sister's wedding. The house's telephone number was Solihull 439 in 1928[62]. That year the Glosters moved to *Holmes House*, Dingle Lane, and later they moved to 516 Streetsbrook Road, which they also named *Sylwood*. Mrs Gloster aged 69 died on 26 December 1951 and was buried on 29 December in St Alphege Churchyard[63]. Probate for her estate, £13,982-6-6d, was granted to her daughters Barbara Grimsley and Kathleen Clarke.

Their successors at No 30 were Theodore Edward Noel and Marjorie THORNLEY[64]. Theodore had been born at Bickenhill in 1876[65] and was recorded in the 1881 Census with his father, Henry aged 67 a retired farmer; mother Emily (45), sister Emily (25) and brother Hugh (4) in Coventry Road, Solihull. Theodore married Marjorie Challens in 1928[66]. She had been born in 1899[67] and so was 23 years younger. At least between 1930 and 1932 they had a maid called Ruby Saunders, but she had left by 1933. On their arrival the telephone number of the house changed to Solihull 571, which became 0571[68]. The 1931/32 Electoral Roll (the last to use house names as opposed to numbers) continued to call the house *Sylwood,* but

[57] *Kelly's Directory for Warwickshire 1908*
[58] *Birth Certificate*
[59] *GRO Index for Q/E September 1940 [Solihull 6d 3397]*
[60] *GRO Index for Q/E June 1917 [Solihull 6d 1335]*
[61] *GRO Index for Q/E June 1940 [Solihull 6d 2822]*
[62] *Kelly's Directory for Warwickshire 1928*
[63] *Burial Records of St Alphege Church*
[64] *Electoral Roll 1929*
[65] *GRO Index for Q/E March 1876 [Meriden 6d 480]*
[66] *GRO Index for Q/E March 1928 [Warwick 6d 985]*
[67] *GRO Index for Q/E September 1899 [Kings Norton 6c 383]*
[68] *Kelly's Directory for Warwickshire 1932*

when Theodore Thornley died aged 60 on 30 October 1936, he was described as of *Marston*, Ashleigh Road. Probate for his estate of £13,870-7-9d was granted to Marjorie his widow, Maurice Isacke Clutterbuck (solicitor) and P.H Stone (chartered accountant).

The house was divided into two flats. Marjorie Thornley, initially with Caroline Key, lived in one; and Francis Edmund and Dorothy Marguerite Challens in the other[69]. Francis Challens was Marjorie's father and Dorothy was his second wife[70] Francis died aged 72 on 28 November 1943 with probate for his estate (£8,973-18-6d) being granted to his widow, Frances Challens spinster (his other daughter), Marjorie Thornley and Maurice Isacke Clutterbuck (solicitor). Victor M.Richmond came to share Dorothy's flat. This continued until at least 1972. Dorothy, whose telephone number in 1955 was Solihull 2854, remained until there her death in 1989[71]. She had been born on 12 February 1891 and so had lived to be 98. She seems to have died intestate as there in no entry in the Will Index between 1989-1991.

After the death of her husband in 1936, Marjorie Thornley was secretary to Albert Stainton (who lived at No 29), by now Treasurer of Solihull Council[72]. She appears to have moved away about 1950. Lilian RANDALL then occupied her flat between 1955-59, followed by Nancy MIDDLETON (1960); Norman & Marina EVANS (1965); Charlotte KNAPP (1970 to 1978); Edith ORCUTT (1979-1984); and Beverley CHIPPENDALE (1984-1989)[73].

In 1989 Brian WHITESIDE of 14 Dovehouse Lane bought the property (telephone number 711 1941) and started converting it back from two flats into a single house. But his wife, Anne Patricia, died unexpectedly on 29 January 1993[74] and his heart went out of the project; he moved with his children to 429 Warwick Road. (Charles) Martin & Sheila STONES moved in and completed the restoration of the house. They have two children – Rebecca (born in 1974) and Nicholas (born in 1976).

### No 32   CLONBEG

Until 1996 when it was demolished, there was a bungalow on this plot which had been designed in 1919/20 by Roland Satchwell & Ernest Roberts, architects & surveyors (but who also practised as estate agents) of 33 Newhall Street, Birmingham. It posed two conundrums. First, because of its construction date, it could not be the property known as *The Bungalow* for which the Electoral Roll listed occupants as early as 1912 (and continuously up to 1927). Second, why was a bungalow built on a full sized plot in a street which otherwise contained expensive two or three storey houses.

The answer to the first mystery was that *The Bungalow* was the initial name of the house now called *Ashleigh House* and numbered 35. The second was addressed by Simon Herrick's research in 1985. The bungalow at No 32 *was built with the aid of a grant under*

---

[69] *Electoral Roll 1939*

[70] *Information from Mr Bill Dewbury*

[71] *GRO Index 1989 [Solihull S. 0789 34 0040]*

[72] *Information from Mr Bill Dewbury*

[73] *Electoral Rolls*

[74] *Probate Index of Wills*

*Front elevation drawing of the original bungalow at No 32 by Satchwell and Roberts, 1919/20.*

the terms of the Housing (Additional Powers) Act 1919. This Act allowed Government money to be paid through Local Authorities towards the construction of houses built by private enterprise. There was no restriction as to who should occupy such houses and the Act did not make special arrangements for disabled or war wounded people. The Act did, nevertheless, limit the size of dwelling and this could partly explain why the bungalow was built. However in a letter from Solihull Council to Satchwell & Roberts, dated 12 February 1920, the Council's surveyor specifically asks for 'certificates from the Ministry of Health' so that 'your case will have attention'. If the client was disabled, then that would precisely explain why the bungalow was built.

The bungalow had a floor to ceiling height of 8ft 6ins which, in a small house, gave its rooms an unusual proportion. Originally the windows were timber mullion & transom, with leaded lights. The walls were rendered above a brick plinth. To the left of the front door there was a hipped gable. There were buttresses on both the left & right of the front elevation, echoing an earlier vogue promoted by C.F.Voisey's country houses of the 1890s[75]. Around 1990 the bungalow's frontage was ruined by a covering of imitation stone and aluminium windows.

The first occupant[76] was Major Walter Brocas LINDESAY who named the house *Clonbeg*. Little is known about him, but he was still alive in 1943 when he acted as executor

[75] *Ashleigh Road Conservation Area by Simon Herrick*
[76] *Kelly's Directory for Warwickshire 1921*

*The bungalow at No 32 after alterations. It was demolished in 1996.*

for the estate (£4,066-1-2d) of Frances Honora Lindesay, spinster (possibly his sister), of Shanklin, Isle of Wight. Major Lindesay did not stay long at *Clonbeg*.

By 1924 Mrs Katherine MORAN was in residence[77]. She lived there by herself until 1928. The 1929 Electoral Roll listed three Morans - Katherine (Kate), Bridget and Mary living in the bungalow. By 1930 the last named had left temporarily. In 1931 Julia, possibly a cousin, arrived. She had been born on 28 October 1908 at 23 Trows Square, Wednesbury, the daughter of Patrick, an iron friddler who made his mark rather than writing his name, and Jane Moran[78]. From 1933 to 1939 all four Morans were in residence. They never had a telephone. After the war Kate, Julia & Mary lived with the Clarkes at No 6.

By 1945 Peter and Alice COMERY lived here, but they did not stay long and did not install a telephone. In 1948 Hubert Hayr and Florence May RYLAND arrived, and they stayed until c1961. Herbert had been born on 3 May 1890 and Florence (nee Morgan) on 10 May 1889. They married in 1915[79]. In 1955 and 1956 Diana K.E.Holiday lived with them, and the telephone number was listed as Solihull 0344 - which remained the number at least into the late 1980s. The Rylands moved to *Celliers,* 5 Langley Road, Claverdon where they both died in 1976 – Florence aged 87 on 26 May worth £3,197 and Hubert aged 86 on 19 September worth £33,257. Thus the Rylands had been born within twelve months of each other and died within six months of the other.

---

[77] *Kelly's Directory for Warwickshire 1924 and Electoral Roll 1924*
[78] *Birth Certificate*
[79] *GRO Index for Q/E December 1915 [Lewisham 1d 3283]*

In 1962 Harold & Edith Beatrice SPOONER came to live in the bungalow. Both had been born in 1897, Harold on 25 August and his wife (nee Jackson) on 4 September. They had married in 1919[80], and their son Leslie was born on 31 December that year. Harold died on 1 February 1973 worth £23,207, and Leslie came to live with his mother. Edith died aged 83 on 23 October 1980; her estate was valued for probate at £44,175. Thereafter Leslie lived in the bungalow by himself until he died on 4 September 1988 at 11 Huntly Road, Edgbaston, worth under £70,000.

After Leslie Spooner died, the property was bought by Patrick KELLY of No 36 who rented the bungalow out[81]. But it deteriorated badly and he had it demolished in 1996 so that he could have a new house built on the site. Designed by John Wood Associates of Wednesbury, work proceeded very slowly due to the illness of the builder (John Traynor of Walsall). The new house bears the date 2000, and is the only house in the road to bear a datestone. Even though not then quite finished, it was first occupied in Autumn 2000. In October 2001 it was advertised for sale and described as having six bedrooms and four bathrooms, besides three reception rooms and a double garage. The purchasers were Ken & Maureen MARSH, with their daughter Ria and her husband Roger BARSBY who came from Stafford – but had had previous connections with Solihull. The Barsbys have a daughter Keziah, known as Kezi, born in 1988.

### No 34   ILFRACOMBE

*This house was designed & built in 1920 by Williams & Boddy, who were builders from Acocks Green. The design is very anachronistic and anyone would be forgiven for estimating it at least ten years earlier. A careful look at the construction, however, shows stretcher bond brickwork which indicates cavity walls. The earlier Ashleigh Road houses are of 9 inch or 13 inch solid construction in Flemish bond. The square front has a three-quarter hipped roof containing a flat roof dormer which is much wider than originally indicated on the drawings. The first floor is rendered between brickwork quoins and to the left of the house is a two storey, five-sided bay window - the radius of which is slightly smaller to the bedroom than to the dining room. This results in a portion of sloped tile hanging at first floor level, which is echoed to the right of the house over the porch - the tiled roof of which tucks under the oriel window above. Woodwork to the porch is very decorative and more characteristic of 1880 than 1920. The house had a China Pantry, and was built with four bedrooms to the first floor and a further bedroom and box room to the attic. Attached to the right hand side is the original 'Motor House'[82].*

Kelly 1921 listed Albert Ernest SHEPPARD at *Ilfracombe*, and the 1922 electoral roll provided the name of his wife - Sophia Elizabeth. They should not be confused with Arthur & Ellen Shepherd who lived at *Glengarth* (No 11) between 1916 & 1922. Albert SHEPPARD lived in the house until about 1972. He had been born on 12 January 1879 and was recorded in the 1881 Census at Belgrave Street, Kings Norton with his parents, Samuel aged 29 a commercial traveller from Marston Magna (Somerset) and Charlotte (28) from

---

[80] *GRO Index for Q/E September 1919 [Birmingham 6d 463]*
[81] *Information from Mr Martin Stones*
[82] *Ashleigh Road Conservation Area by Simon Herrick*

*No 34 in 2002. It was designed by Williams and Boddy in 1920.*

Clerkenwell. Sophia died aged only 53 on 27 March 1932 and probate for her estate (£2,682-14-2d) was granted to Albert, who was described as a brassfounder. They had a son Raymond, born on 23 April 1907, who was listed in the 1930 electoral roll, along with Margaret Alice Johnson, presumably a servant. In 1931 there was a second servant, Elsie Lovatt, but she had disappeared by 1933 leaving Albert and Raymond with Margaret Johnson to look after them. That year[83], on 20 September at Knowle Parish Church, Raymond married Florence Lancaster of No 25 Ashleigh Road. He had become a brassfounder, like his father, and with his new bride went to live at Dorridge. Later they moved to 11 Poplar Close, Oversley Green near Alcester where, ten years after the death of his wife, Raymond died on 5 March 1992 worth £171,645.

Albert married again in 1937[84]. His bride was Dorothy Pattie Treves. The 1938 Electoral Roll listed them both but Margaret Johnson no longer lived with them. In 1946 their servant was Lily Edmonds, but she had disappeared by 1950. The 1949 directory listed a telephone for the first time - Solihull 2295. Albert drove a Rover car, but always in the middle of the road - much to the consternation of other traffic[85]. Now described as a retired master brassfounder, he became a widower for the second time when Dorothy died on 10 March

---

[83] *Marriage Certificate*
[84] *GRO Index for Q/E December 1937 [Solihull 6d 2075]*
[85] *Information from Mr Bill Dewbury*

1964 at 384 Tessall Lane, Northfield, with an estate of £2,425. Thereafter Albert lived alone and kindly Mrs Patterson from No 35 would regularly call in to see how he was. Unfortunately he did not appreciate this as much as he should have done[86]. In 1972 he moved into a nursing home at 38 Warwick New Road, Leamington where he died four days after his 95th birthday on 16 January 1974 worth £102,073. He was buried alongside his first wife in Robin Hood Cemetery.

John A. and Jean M. HIGGINS were listed in the 1973 Electoral Roll, with their son Peter G. (who reached voting age on 23 January that year). They retained the 2295 telephone number and stayed until 1977. Michael & Penelope WINTERBORN were the next occupants: they remained until 1986, when Graham & Caroline CLAYTON, both teachers, arrived. Since 1997[87] Caroline has lived in the house with her children, Tomos (born 1986) and Jenny (born 1988).

## No 36   WAVERTREE / SAPPHIRE HOUSE

*A white, rendered, two storey house of the 1920s. It, like the bungalow previously at No 32, has a buttressed elevation. Its hipped roof comes almost to a point - although the pitch of the roof and the front gable is low. There is a 5 sided front window with a dentil mould to the eaves[88].*

George BENTON was the first occupant, and he called his house *Wavertree*[89]. He had been born in 1879 and was shown in the 1881 Census at 12 Cromwell Street Aston with his parents, John aged 36 a brass dresser, and Eliza (22) a pearl button finisher. George married Margaret Emily[90]. By October 1924 [91]they had moved to a house in Broad Oaks Road, which they also called *Wavertree*.

The Ashleigh Road house was occupied by Henry and Dora WOOD, with two of their children Leonard and Emily, who had moved down the road from No 3 which they had sold in November 1923. Henry, a tinsmith, died aged 69 on 5 December 1924 leaving an estate of only £54-19-6d. Nine months later, on 30 September 1925, Leonard, a mechanical engineer aged 26, married Kate Emily May Fitch at Birmingham South Register Office[92]. She was a milliner aged 21, the daughter of John William Fitch, of independent means, who lived at 45 Smallbrook Street, Birmingham. Dora continued to live at *Wavertree* with Emily until 1928, when they moved to 74 Silhill Hall Road[93]. Mrs Wood died there on 12 February 1943 worth £15,913-6-3d. Her executors were her son Leonard, described as a works manager, and John Stanley William Miller, traveller.

John Arnold and Dora Winifred JUCKES lived in the house from at least 1929[94] and

---

[86] *Ibid*
[87] *Electoral Roll 1997*
[88] *Ashleigh Road Conservation Area by Simon Herrick*
[89] *Kelly's Directory for Warwickshire 1921*
[90] *Electoral Roll 1922*
[91] *Electoral Roll 1924*
[92] *Marriage Certificate*
[93] *Electoral Roll 1928*
[94] *Electoral Roll 1929*

stayed until 1934 but never installed a telephone (although John had one at his office at 86 Snow Hill, Birmingham). Later in life they lived at *West Mount,* Middlefield Lane, Hagley, where John died aged 64 on 9 September 1951. Probate for his estate was given to his widow.

They were succeeded in that year by Thomas and Mary DUNN, with their servant Jane Ann McDonough. Their telephone number was Solihull 0594. Thomas came from Scotland and became the manager in Birmingham for the Royal Sun Alliance Insurance Society. His brother became his equivalent in Coventry[95]. The Dunns, who were fervent Roman Catholics[96], had four children: Winifred (who was shown on the electoral rolls from 1934 to 1939), (Theresa) Jane (1934-39), Mary (1936-66) and John G. (1936-59). Jane McDonough had disappeared by 1950. Thomas died aged 75 on 14 November 1951, and probate for his estate (£846-0-4d) was granted to his widow, Mary Ann Dunn. She stayed in the house with her daughter Mary and her son John. The latter had left home by 1960. Mrs Dunn died aged 88 on 3 February 1965 at Selly Oak Hospital, probate for her estate (£658) being granted to her youngest daughter. Mary then lived in the house by herself until 1984.

The middle daughter, Jane, had been born on 17 August 1912. She married a Mr KELLY and had Patrick and Una. After her husband's death, she and the children took over the house from her sister Mary Dunn. Una married Alan K.Wilson in 1985[97]. Jane died in 1990[98]. Jane's son, Patrick Kelly, who was the head teacher in a Birmingham school, continued to live there by himself until 1997. After Leslie Spooner of No 32 (the bungalow) died in 1988, Patrick bought that property and eventually redeveloped the site. In order to fund that project, Patrick moved out of No 36[99], which he had renamed *Sapphire House,* in 1996. His successors were Timothy & Laura O'CONNELL, but they stayed only two years. In 1998 Stuart & Anne METCALF came to live in the house. They put it on the market in September 2001.

### No 38   JESMOND DENE

Simon Herrick wrote in 1985: *'No 38 was designed in June 1922 by H.Peter Hing who at that time was at 121 Colmore Row, Birmingham. Research has shown that Peter Hing joined E.H.Wigley in 1906 as a young architectural apprentice. At that time he was 21. Conceivably, Peter Hing could have been involved at some subsidiary level with Numbers 1 and 16 & 18. It has already been noted that the practice of Peter Hing & Jones designed No 28A in 1954. But the thirty years that lie between Nos 38 & 28A did not in fact manifest any great architectural leaps between them. In fact the earlier house is rather more convincing than its stable mate, but neither of them breaks any new ground and neither offends any of the Ashleigh Road principles in the way that John Surman's No 37 did so successfully in 1927.*

*No 38 was in fact designed for Mr Harvey Butterworth, a 'Manufacturing Jeweller'. It is of brickwork, render & timber, and has a gabled & timbered entrance bay in the centre, and a further projecting bay to the right of that. The plan incorporates a China Pantry*

---

[95] *Information from Mr Patrick Kelly*
[96] *Information from Mrs Josephine Warden (nee Woodfield)*
[97] *GRO Index for 1985 [Solihull S 0685 34 0233]*
[98] *GRO Index for 1990 [Solihull S 0590 34 0138]*
[99] *Information from Mr Martin Stones*

*East elevation drawing of No 38 by Peter Hing. It was built in 1922.*

*adjacent to the kitchen, and as part of the hall there is a 'Bay Seat' which is just to the left of the porch. Upstairs there are 3 bedrooms, a bathroom & a very tiny box room. The latter clearly was not a priority here as it had been in some of the earlier and larger houses. With 8ft 6ins floor to ceiling heights upstairs and down, the proportions of the elevations are immediately pleasing & reasonable. Hing obviously considered the corner plot more seriously the De Lacy-Aherne did at No 20. In doing so he created not only a fine front to Ashleigh Road but also a thoughtful side elevation to Streetsbrook Road, which has a two-storey bay window'.*

 (Richard) Harvey and Eileen Ann BUTTERWORTH were shown in the 1924 Electoral Roll and lived in the house, which they named *Jesmond Dene* (perhaps they had once lived in that district of Newcastle-upon-Tyne), until 1929. Jessie Butterworth was with them in the latter year. Harvey had been born in 1861[100], the eldest son of Thomas Butterworth, a clerk. He had two brothers and a sister. His father had married secondly Catherine Hancox and, with her two sons, the whole family was shown in the 1881 Census at 67 Wills Street, Aston. Harvey was described as a 'gem setter (gold)'. He married Eliza on 6 August 1881 at St Thomas, Birmingham. She was the daughter of Edward Adderley, a gun maker[101]. Harvey &

---

[100] *GRO Index for Q/E June 1861 [Dudley 6a 60]*
[101] *Marriage Certificate*

*Cartoon of Peter Hing
(1885-1961)*

Eliza had a daughter, Jessie, who was born in 1882[102]. She died aged only 48 in 1931[103]. Towards the end of his life Harvey, presumably with his wife, moved to 18 Totterdown Road, Weston-super-Mare, where he died aged 80 on 16 August 1941 leaving £2,706-14-3d. Probate was granted to Beatrice Mabel Badger, the wife of Leo Austin Badger.

From 1930 there was a 30 year period of short occupancies and times when the house did not appear to be occupied at all. Llewelyn Caradoc EVANS and his wife Nellie were in residence from 1930 to 1932. In 1933[104] Reginald and Dorothy MATTINSON, with Winifred Lee, lived in the house. But it was for that year only since in 1934 it was empty. In 1935 Joseph W.SMITH was the occupant[105], with a telephone (Solihull 0896), but the 1936 & 1937 electoral rolls listed Jack and Kathleen SMITH. Frederick and Mary Bridget WRIGHT were the occupants in 1938. The house was empty in 1939 and the electoral rolls then have no entry for it until 1955, when James Stanley WHITLEY & Margaret Joyce MOODY were shown.

---

[102] *GRO Index for Q/E December 1882 [Aston 6d 367]*
[103] *GRO Index for Q/E March 1931 [Birmingham N 6d 639]*
[104] *Electoral Roll 1933*
[105] *Telephone Directory 1935*

By late 1958 William & Nancy Marjorie CARTWRIGHT had come to live in the house, and it emerged from its long period of short term - or no - occupants. The Cartwrights installed a telephone (Solihull 5673). They seem to have had a daughter, Carole, who appeared in the 1965-67 Electoral Rolls and a son Paul, who was listed in 1973. He became a merchant seaman, and was shown as such until 1985. William died on 8 January 1989 with an estate of £15,841. Thereafter Nancy Cartwright lived in the house by herself. She died in 1998[106], having been born on 24 September 1919. The house was bought by John GREEN of Silhill Hall Road who leases it out to tenants. There have been no entries in the 1999-2001 electoral rolls.

---

[106] *GRO Index for 1998 [Birmingham 0611P P5B 096 0298]*

# 7. HOUSES 23 TO 39

## No 23    EDSTON / THE MANSE.

Semi-detached with No 25, the pair feature high, rendered gables flanked by impressive 'cat-slide' roofs which sweep down to first floor level. Each house has two storey bays, with four bay windows, and casements to the second floor bedrooms above. At the rear the two are not quite identical, No 23 having a small porch in the centre of the ground floor bay which extends along the whole length of the house, and its side outbuildings do not protrude beyond this. The rear elevation has a distinctive course line in the brickwork of the unusually large gap between the top of the first, and the bottom of the second floor windows. This suggests that the original intention may have been to have had a lower roof line at the rear, possibly with dormer windows.

The houses were built in 1905/6 on land purchased from Joseph Albert Wells by Thomas & Arthur LANCASTER, sons of Martin Thomas Lancaster who was the first occupant of No 23. Originally there was no fencing between the houses[1] as both belonged to, and were occupied by, members of the Lancaster family.

Martin was the eldest of eight children of Thomas Lancaster and his wife Rebecca Billings who had married at St Mary the Virgin, Lapworth on 17 December 1835. He was baptised in that church on 15 May 1839 and married Ann Lewis on 21 July 1862 at St Peter, Wootton Wawen[2]. She had been born about 1841 at Henley-in-Arden. They were recorded in the 1881 Census living at 118 Bath Row, Birmingham with their daughter Laura (16, no occupation) and son Martin Lewis (10, scholar). They also had five lodgers, of whom four were operatic artists and one a Divisional Officer of Excise. Martin was then described as a book binder, but later he became a printer's foreman[3].

He was one of only 10 voters recorded as living in Ashleigh Road in the 1907 electoral roll. His wife died on 9 February 1908: probate for her estate, £308-7-1d, was granted to his sons, Martin Lewis & Arthur Leslie Lancaster, described as printers' travellers. Martin Thomas remained in residence until his death, aged 72, on 9 February 1911. He was buried, with his wife Ann, in St Alphege churchyard. Probate for his estate, £2,203-4-7d, was granted to Martin Lewis & Arthur Leslie Lancaster. The latter lived next door at No 25.

Miss Laura LANCASTER (Martin's daughter) was living in the house by 1912[4]. She remained until 1939, having Sarah Ann Hughes - a servant or companion - living with her from at least 1929. She never had a telephone installed. Miss Lancaster moved to 91 Tilehouse Green Lane, Bentley Heath, where she died on 8 May 1949, aged 86, a month after

---

[1] *Information from the Rev'd David Blanchflower*
[2] *International Genealogical Index*
[3] *Probate Index of Wills*
[4] *Kelly's Directory for Warwickshire 1912*

*Nos 23 and 25 in 2002. A semi-detached pair with cat-slide roofs, built 1905/6. No 23 has an air-raid shelter beneath the front garden.*

her brother Arthur. Her funeral took place at St Alphege on 11 May[5]. Probate for her estate (£506-4-2d) was granted to Martin Lewis Lancaster, now a master printer. As so many of the Lancaster family lived in Ashleigh Road, their genealogical tree is shown in Appendix IV.

By 1940[6] Edgar Henry & Gladys BANNISTER lived in the house. They appear to have rented it from the Lancasters. Edgar had been born on 23 October 1899. He married Gladys Beddows in 1922[7]. She died during the Second World War, and Edgar married Barbara Deans in 1946[8]. The electoral rolls show them in residence between 1947-57, with Edgar's son by his first marriage, Anthony Edgar Bannister (born 1930[9]), from 1952-57. The 1949 telephone directory listed the number as Solihull 2381. The Bannisters moved to *Maryland,* Sherborne Road, Bourton-on-the-Water, where Edgar died on 30 January 1977 leaving £1,625.

The house was purchased on 9 June 1958 by the Birmingham Elmdon Circuit, as a manse for the Methodist Minister, from Mrs Bessie Lancaster, widow, of 25 Ashleigh Road for £3625.

---

[5] *Burial Records of St Alphege Church*
[6] *Kelly's Directory for Warwickshire 1940*
[7] *GRO Index for Q/E September 1922 [Chorlton 8c 2019]*
[8] *GRO Index for Q/E December 1946 [Solihull 9c 2148]*
[9] *GRO Index for Q/E September 1930 [Manchester S 8d 96]*

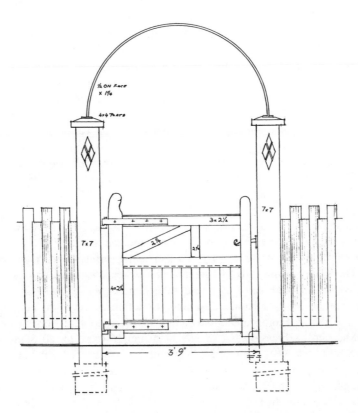

*Design for the front gate of No 23 from the original blueprint. The left hand pillar, with its distinctive decoration, still remains.*

The Rev'd (Edward) Gordon DAVIES was the first Minister to occupy the new manse (which replaced a large gabled 3 storey manse with eight bedrooms at 67 New Road) in August 1958. He was delighted with the greenhouse which contained a vine, and with the large pear tree whose luscious fruit was useful when making hospital visits[10]. His wife was called Tess. Their telephone number was Solihull 1392, which remains the number today.

In August 1963 they were succeeded by the Rev'd Brian GREET and his wife Jill. In August 1972 the Rev'd Ronald RICH and his wife Judith, with their son Jonathan (born 29 October 1956), became the occupants. Apart from his ministerial duties, he wrote scripts for Frank Muir & Denis Norden, and took part when the former was the subject of *This is Your Life* on television[11].

The Rev'd Bernard DOWDING was the next Minister to occupy *The Manse*, from August 1977, with his wife Gillian and daughters Susan (born 13 July 1960) & Heather (born 7 March 1963). The Rev'd John LLOYD WILLIAMS arrived in 1982. Normally

[10] *His recollections in 'Travelling On' by Edna Handley, 1997*
[11] *Information from the Rev'd David Blanchflower*

Methodist Ministers stay for at least five years, but Mr Lloyd Williams was appointed Chaplain to Homes for the Aged in 1986. His American born wife was also a minister and was involved with the establishment of the joint Anglican & Methodist local ecumenical project on the new Monkspath estate. She officiated at Solihull Methodist Church as well for the gap year. They had a daughter Alison, born 9 September 1969.

The Rev'd Peter & Susan BATES came in August 1988 with their son Richard (born 9 June 1977), and stayed until 1995. It was only during their time that the outbuilding close to the rear of No 25 which impinged into *The Manse's* garden was demolished, thus allowing the boundary fence to be straightened. In 1994 the end (90ft length approximately) of their rear garden was sold to No 37 The Crescent. The present minister is the Rev'd David BLANCHFLOWER, with his wife Jennifer. They have two adult sons, Peter & Sean.

## No 25    THE DEN

Stanley EVERED, like his neighbour, was one of the first residents in Ashleigh Road[12]. He was almost certainly a tenant of Martin Lancaster, and had left by 1909.

Arthur Leslie LANCASTER, Martin's son and a printer's traveller, was the next occupant[13] He had been born in 1881[14] and married Florence Emma Dixon on 14 November 1906 at St Nicholas, Baddesley Ensor near Atherstone. Aged 29, she was a schoolteacher and the daughter of George Dixon, a coalminer. Both fathers signed the marriage certificate as witnesses. Arthur & Florence had two daughters. Florence Vera, born in 1908[15], married Raymond Sheppard, a brassfounder of No 34 Ashleigh Road, on 20 September 1933 at Knowle Parish Church. They went to live in Dorridge, but towards the end of their lives lived at *Woodside,* 11 Poplar Close, Oversley Green, near Alcester, where she died on 13 April 1982 worth not more than £25,000. Edna Leila was born in 1912[16] and married Ivor M.Price in 1935[17]. Mrs Lancaster died on 8 December 1933 with probate for her estate, £450-13-1d, being granted to her husband, now described as a printer.

Arthur married secondly Bessie Cowley in 1939[18], and she appeared as Bessie Lancaster on the electoral rolls for the first time in 1945, there having been none during the war. Aged 67, Arthur died on 8 April 1949 worth £17,394-19-7d and was buried in St Alphege churchyard. They had a telephone as early as 1924[19] - Solihull 148, which became 0148 with the introduction of 4 figure numbers in 1931 and remains the number today. The Lancasters were keen astronomers and had a large telescope in the thatched outbuilding at the rear of their house[20]. That outbuilding was not demolished until the early 1990s. At the start of the

---

[12] *Electoral Roll 1907; and Kelly's Directory for Warwickshire 1908,*
     *but spelt Everhard therein*
[13] *Electoral Roll 1910*
[14] *GRO Index for Q/E September 1881 [Birmingham 6d 77]*
[15] *GRO Index for Q/E June 1908 [Solihull 6d 648]*
[16] *GRO Index for Q/E March 1912 [Solihull 6d 1229]*
[17] *GRO Index for Q/E September 1935 [Solihull 6d 2579]*
[18] *GRO Index for Q/E September 1939 [Birmingham 6d 1524]*
[19] *Kelly's Directory for Warwickshire 1924*
[20] *Information from the Rev'd David Blanchflower*

Second World War an air raid shelter was constructed under the front lawn, with a ventilation shaft beside the front wall. The shelter was accessed from the cellar under the house, and still exists.

Bessie LANCASTER had been born on 31 May 1902, and was described as a widow in June 1958 when she sold No 23 to the Methodist Church. She remained in No 25, often by herself, until her death in 1995. Her son Alastair (born in 1940[21]) was sent as a boarder to Eversfield School despite it being only 450 yards away. He was shown with her in the 1962-65 and 1968 Electoral Rolls. He married Sylvia Bird in 1972[22]. In 1974, for that year only, he & Sylvia lived with Bessie. In 1978 he returned by himself, presumably after his divorce. He also lived in the house from 1993 until 1996 - the latter year with his son, David – and then went to live in Aberystwyth.

The Lancasters occupied this house for 87 years, from 1909 until 1996, the longest connection of any family with Ashleigh Road. Their nearest competitors are the Dewburys at No 33, whose occupation since 1928 still continues.

Angus and Helen GRAY came to live in the house in September 1996. They have Ben and Daniel. Angus is the fleet sales manager of MG Rover. His father, an Edinburgh architect, has produced a beautiful picture record of No 25 with plans and many photographs, both of the house originally and now, and also of the Lancaster family.

## No 27   THORPE COTTAGE

*Although it has a small amount of applied timber framing, the whole front elevation is far less flamboyant than some of its more illustrious neighbours further up the road[23].* The flat roof of the extension was somewhat out of sympathy with the rest of the house, but was replaced with a pitched roof in 2001.

The first occupant in 1908 was Gustavus William USHER[24]. Born in 1865, he was the eldest of eight children of Samuel, a jeweller, and Sarah Usher of 85 Camden Street, Birmingham[25]. Gustavus became a manufacturing jeweller and from Vicarage Road, Handsworth married Annie Holmes on 19 May 1892 at Hamstead Road Baptist Church[26]. A year younger than him, Annie was the daughter of William James Holmes, a wholesale jeweller. They had a son, Wilfrid Holmes Usher, born in 1893[27], but sadly Annie died aged only 31 in 1897[28]. On 19 June 1901 Gustavus, now living at 18 Radnor Road, married Sarah Caroline Gatheral at St Michael, Handsworth. Aged 26, she was the daughter of George Gatheral, a chemist of Patshull House, Soho Road, Handsworth[29]. The 1924 electoral roll listed Gustavus & Sarah in Ashleigh Road, together with Wilfrid. The telephone

---

[21] *GRO Index for Q/E June 1940 Birmingham 6d 832*

[22] *GRO Index for Q/E June 1972 [Birmingham 9c 906]*

[23] *Ashleigh Road Conservation Area by Simon Herrick*

[24] *Electoral Roll 1908*

[25] *1881 Census*

[26] *Marriage Certificate*

[27] *GRO Index for Q/E September 1893 [West Bromwich 6b 814]*

[28] *GRO Index for Q/E June 1897 [Solihull 6d 338]*

[29] *Marriage Certificate*

(Solihull 356) was installed after 1924 but before 1928[30]. The Ushers remained at *Thorpe Cottage* for 23 years; by 1931 they had moved to *'Fairoaks'*, 473 Streetsbrook Road. Gustavus died there on 1 January 1952, aged 86, worth £1,360-0-7d, and Sarah on 12 December 1956 (£4,138-12-5d), the executor in each case being Lloyds Bank.

Bertram Kent PARSONS and his wife Muriel Evelyn nee Lonnen arrived in 1930, and the telephone number was changed to Solihull 0261. Bertram was born on 12 May 1892 and had married Muriel in 1915[31]. They had a son called Geoffrey Kent who was born on 2 September 1917 at Penrhos Lodge, Conway Road, Colwyn Bay[32]. Bertram was then described as a Captain 2/8 Battalion, the Warwickshire Regiment. The family stayed in the house until the middle of the Second World War. Eventually they moved to 6 Broadway Road, Torquay, where Bertram died aged 83 on 23 February 1976, worth £9,965.

By 1945[33] Dr Noel Trelawney GLYNN and his wife Christina, also a doctor, had taken up residence. They kept the same telephone number as their predecessors (0261). Christine Gibson lived with them, although by 1946 she had been replaced by Edith M.Adams and in 1955 by Margaret Annie Brown. The Glynns had two sons. Thomas Hugh became a seaman and was shown as such on the 1956 & 1957 electoral rolls. John was listed on the rolls between 1965 and 1970.

Dr Noel GLYNN (who had been born on 15 February 1899) was the Company doctor for many years at Land Rover or at Longbridge[34]. He was crippled by arthritis until the drug cortisone was available, when he was able to resume work[35]. The Glynns stayed at No 27 until Christina (who had been born on 12 December 1904) died in 1979[36]. Noel then moved to 129 Touchwood Hall Close, where he died on 29 July 1985 worth £158,481.

They were succeeded by Graham & Christine HUGHES. They had a son, and two daughters - Emma who became 18 on 4 April 1990, and Katherine on 24 March 1992. Their telephone number was 705 4290, which remains the number today. Graham Hughes was a giftware manufacturer and became a Governor of Solihull School (of which he was an old boy, as was his son)[37]. They moved to Netherwood Heath Farmhouse, Baddesley Clinton.

By 1994 David & Suzanne READ had come to live in the house, and they are still there. In 2001 they extended the house at the rear and placed a pitched roof on the original side extension.

**No 29    VILETTE**
This is one of only five houses in the road which still displays its original name. It *has a three storey gabled bay to the right and a two storey bay to the left. The three storey bay has a five sided window to the ground floor front room, with casements above. The two storey*

---

[30] *Kelly's Directory for Warwickshire 1928*
[31] *GRO Index for Q/E September 1915 [Birmingham 6d 768]*
[32] *Birth Certificate*
[33] *Electoral Roll 1945*
[34] *Mr Sansbury thinks the former, and Mr Dewbury thinks the latter*
[35] *Information from Mr Bill Dewbury*
[36] *GRO Index for Q/E March 1979 [Solihull S. 34 0118]*
[37] *Information from Mr Michael Sansbury*

*bay has a semi-circular entrance to the recessed porch, and an oriel window tucked under the deeply overhanging eaves. At first floor level there is a dentil-mould string course, above which the facade is rendered, apart from a suggestion of tile hanging high up in the eaves of the gable. It was built in about 1905/6*[38].

The house's first occupant was Albert STAINTON[39]. The 1881 Census had listed him as a scholar aged 12, the youngest of six children (all born in Birmingham) of Samuel (50) & Mary (52) Stainton of 39 Pershore Road, Edgbaston. Samuel was a hosier whose three elder daughters were assisting in his shop. From Princess Road, Edgbaston, Albert - described as the Assistant Clerk to the Guardians (of Solihull) - married Sarah Louisa Field at St Bartholemew, Edgbaston on 11 July 1894. Aged 22, she was the daughter of William Field, a cab proprietor of Sparkbrook[40]. They lived at Sharmans Cross[41] and had two sons. Carl Rodney was born in 1896[42] and lived with them until 1931[43]; and Clement Alfred who was born in 1904[44]. There was also a daughter called Marjorie. They lived at *Vilette* beyond Albert's death in 1945 but never had a telephone installed.

Kelly's Directory described Albert Stainton in 1916 as the Assistant Overseer & Collector of Poor Rates at The Rates Office, Warwick Road; and in 1921 as the Assistant Overseer & Clerk to Solihull Parish Council at Park Road. He died on 19 October 1945 at the Queen Elizabeth Hospital, Edgbaston, leaving an estate of £3,079-8-2d. His widow continued to live in the house with a companion, Dorothy Coxon[45]. Sarah Stainton died aged 81 in 1953[46]. The Staintons thus occupied the house for 46 years but this does not match the Petries at No 21 (1908-73), the Lancasters at No 25 (1909-96), and the Dewburys at No 33 (1928 to date).

Roy George & Vera Frances SNODIN were listed as the occupants in the 1955 Electoral Roll and stayed until after 1965. They installed a telephone, Solihull 4044, which remains the number today. By 1968 Wilfrid and Patricia BUTT had come to live in the house, with their companion Julia P.Sharp. Professor Butt was an endocrinologist at Birmingham University. Their son John (born 17 November 1960) attended Solihull School and was a fine musician, becoming organ scholar of King's College, Cambridge in the early 1980s. After gaining a PhD there, he went to Aberdeen University (where he married) and Berkeley University, California, before returning to Cambridge where he is now a Fellow of Kings College[47]. Wilfred & Patricia, who also had a daughter Susan (born 4 July 1952), stayed in the house until 1986 when they moved to Stratford-on-Avon.

They were succeeded by David & Janet SPILSBURY, with Philip & Andrew. The latter was 18 on 3 May 1987. They are still there, although their sons have now left home.

---

[38] *Ashleigh Road Conservation Area by Simon Herrick*
[39] *Kelly's Directory for Warwickshire 1908*
[40] *Marriage Certificate*
[41] *Electoral Rolls 1902 & 1905*
[42] *GRO Index for Q/E December 1896 [Aston 6d 262]*
[43] *Electoral Rolls*
[44] *GRO Index for Q/E December 1904 [Solihull 6d 635]*
[45] *Electoral Roll 1950*
[46] *GRO Index for Q/E December 1953 [Solihull 9c 856]*
[47] *Information from Mr David Turnbull*

*Nos 31 and 33 in 2002, a pair of semi-detached houses designed by E.H. Wigley and built in 1910.*

## No 31   THE NEWLANDS

The Borough Conservation Architect in 1985 wrote *'Nos 31 & 33 are a pair of double gabled houses which, because of their massing, look almost like a terrace of four. Black & white to number 31 and blue & white to 33, however, soon gives the game away. They are joined at their timbered bays. The first floor forms a jetty over the ground floor. This arrangement derives of course from mediaeval precedents. In view of Ashleigh Road's flirtation - albeit superficial - with the English timber framed tradition, it is surprising that the jetty only occurs here and at No 35, and in an extremely eccentric form at No 14. Traditionally it was a status symbol and that is why it is employed here with such convincing architectural effect.*

*The other gabled windows project forward slightly and have rectangular bay windows at ground & first floor with leaded-light casements and a tiled, pitched roof. No 14 was designed by E.H.Wigley but the use of leaded lights, the roof over the bay windows and the triangular oriel window found at 31 & 33 are not part of the Wigley vocabulary. Numbers 31 & 33 and 14 do have jetties but this does not seem sufficient evidence to attribute 31 & 33 to Wigley. Nevertheless this pair, with garages to match, stand as a worthy epitaph to another anonymous Edwardian Architect of considerable skill.'* In fact Ernest Wigley did design this pair of houses[48].

---

[48] *Information from Mr Bill Dewbury*

The first occupant[49] was George Frederick BULL and his family who, in 1911, installed the second telephone in the road (the first was at No 14 in 1908): its number was Solihull 49[50]. He had been shown, a scholar of 13, in the 1881 Census with his family at 20 Melen Street, Redditch. His father, aged 44, was a needle scourer; his mother was 47, and they had five children. The eldest Kate, a dressmaker aged 24, was married to William Avery, a clerk of 20, and they lived with the Bull family. George had another elder sister, besides two younger ones.

George married Sarah Jane Fletcher in 1891[51] and they had four daughters. Doris Eugenie was born in 1893[52], and married Harold William Stockbridge in 1915[53]. Gwendoline Charlotte was born on 12 June 1895 at Rednall Villa, Bournbrook, Northfield[54]; she married Thomas R.Duff in 1918[55], but sadly had been widowed by the time her father died in 1933; Constance was born in 1896[56] and married Thomas Basley Boal; and Zelie Georgina, born on 3 June 1904 at 47 Tennyson Avenue, Aston[57].

George was described as a draughtsman in 1895 and as a cycle works manager in 1904, but by the time the family lived in Ashleigh Road he was a director of the ATCO lawnmower company[58]. When Constance was 17 and Zelie eight, their mother died aged only 37 in 1913. George married again: after the Bulls moved to Longdon Croft, Copt Heath, the 1920 electoral roll showed his wife's name as Lilian. George died aged 65 on 29 April 1933. Probate for his estate, £49,296-15-5d, was granted to his four daughters. Zelie remained unmarried. She became a teacher and was one of the co-founders of St Martins School[59]. She conducted elocution lessons during the 1930s in a room above Mary Mary's, a children's clothes shop in the High Street[60]. In later life she lived at 12 Alderbrook Road, where she died on 23 September 1964 worth £4,279.

They were succeeded before 1921[61] by Frederick Linney BARBER, who lived at *The Newlands* with his wife Emily Agnes and son, Eric. Frederick had been born at Bromsgrove in 1872, the third son of William & Sarah Barber. He was recorded in the 1881 Census as a scholar living with his family of four brothers and five sisters at 82 Belmont Row, Aston. Frederick married Emily in 1896[62] and Eric was born in 1898[63]. Described as a

---

[49] *Electoral Roll 1910*

[50] *Birmingham & District Telephone Directory*

[51] *GRO Index for Q/E December 1891 [Foleshill 6d 883]*

[52] *GRO Index for Q/E June 1893 [Coventry 6d 551]*

[53] *GRO Index for Q/E March 1915 [Solihull 6d 1091]*

[54] *Birth Certificate*

[55] *GRO Index for Q/E March 1918 [Solihull 6d 1352]*

[56] *GRO Index for Q/E September 1896 [Kings Norton 6c 428]*

[57] *Birth Certificate*

[58] *Information from Mr Bill Dewbury*

[59] *Ibid*

[60] *Information from Mrs Diana Mitchell MBE*

[61] *Kelly's Directory for Warwickshire 1921*

[62] *GRO Index for Q/E September 1896 [Kidderminster 6c 328]*

[63] *GRO Index for Q/E September 1898 [W Bromwich 6b 894]*

furniture manufacturer, Frederick died aged only 50 on 23 March 1922 worth £4,013-11s. Emily & Eric were listed in the October 1923 electoral roll, but they must have left soon after that as Kelly's Directory 1924 contains no entry for *The Newlands*.

The 1927-29 Electoral Rolls listed Frederick George Sydney and Hilda Gladys May CROWTHER, with Lillian Dorothy Sidwell - presumably their servant. The Crowthers had married on 14 June 1910 at Holy Trinity, Birchfield[64].

Harold Charles and Emma Elsie PHIPPS came to live in the house in 1930 and stayed for four years. They reinstalled a telephone - Solihull 699 which, with the introduction of four figure numbers in 1931, became 0699. They had two servants, or lodgers, to start with - Millicent Annie Hawkins & Dora Lake - which had become three by October 1933 - Ada Wilson, May Wesson & Alice Hetherington[65].

By October 1934 John William BRYAN was in residence with his wife Mabel, and their servant Frances Ellison. The Bryans had a daughter[66] and their telephone number was Solihull 0975. John was Sales Director for the Birmingham Small Arms Company. The family remained in the house until late 1944, and were therefore in residence for most of World War II. This must have been a worrying time for them as the BSA factory in Small Heath was essential to the war effort and a target for German bombs. It made bicycles as well as rifles, using the same technology for the tubes.

In 1945 Norman P. & Doris Mary LESTER, with Ellen Speakman as their servant arrived, but they did stay long as the house was empty in 1946. They did not have a telephone. He later became Town Clerk of Solihull. Early in 1947 Mrs Ellen E.KIRK (a widow) & Alice LEWIS took up residence, initially with Edith Wylde. They reinstated the telephone (Solihull 2733) and stayed until 1963. In 1964, for one year only, Mr & Mrs HAYNES, with a child remembered as being badly behaved, lived in the house[67].

The new owners in 1965 were John & Joan BLACK The telephone number changed to Solihull 4131, and by 1970[68] they had been joined by Ethel A.Knight, Joan's mother. John Alexander Black, who became well known in the advertising world, had been born in Sheffield in 1923, educated at Cheltenham College, and then entered his father's business A.A.Black Ltd (of which he was a director 1948-63). He married Joan Knight and they had two daughters, (Cynthia) Anne (born 18 January 1952, now Mrs Botterill) and Amanda Alison (born 16 July 1956, now Mrs Congreave). At the time he was living in Ashleigh Road, John was also a director of Photographic Arts Ltd and Longleys & Hoffman Ltd - of which he became Managing Director in 1972 when it was taken over by the Charles Barker Group Ltd. John was Chairman of the Midlands Branch of The Institute of Practioners in Advertising, and President of the Birmingham Chamber of Industry & Commerce in 1981/82. He also served on numerous public bodies, eg the Birmingham Council of Social Service 1960-74; Commissioners for Income Tax 1966-72; and Solihull Health Authority 1974-89[69]. He was

---

[64] *Marriage Certificate*
[65] *Electoral Roll 1933*
[66] *Information from Mr Bill Dewbury*
[67] *Ibid*
[68] *Electoral Roll 1970*
[69] *Birmingham Year Book 1991*

appointed CBE in 1983, and six years later retired to his native Sheffield where he died on 28 October 2001[70].

In 1974 the Blacks moved to 36 Hampton Lane, taking Solihull 4131 with them. They sold the Ashleigh Road house to Malcolm & Janet GARDNER who refitted the kitchen & bathroom, and stayed until 1980 when they moved to No 12.

Dr John & Anne BEAL bought the property for £62,500[71]. He was the Area Dental Officer for Birmingham and had come from Nailsea (Somerset), having lived previously in Raddington Drive, Olton[72]. They moved in on 28 August 1980 with two of their children - Nicholas (born on 27 September 1971, now a solicitor with the Yorkshire Building Society) and Rebecca (born 25 July 1974, now a teacher in North Yorkshire) - who both attended Oak Cottage School. Hannah was born in the house on 7 February 1982, a cold frosty morning, and is now training as an occupational therapist in York[73]. The telephone number of the house was 704 1462. The Beals sold the property for £69,500[74] and left on 26 April 1984. They moved to Leeds where John had secured another Health Service appointment.

Jonathan & Elizabeth WOODWARD were the new owners. Liz was the widow of Dr Thompson, a Shirley GP who sadly died early by his own hand[75]. She had then married Jonathan in 1982[76]. Living with them were Claire Thompson, who attained the age of 18 on 25 January 1987 and remained until 1990, and Guy Thompson[77]. These were presumably the children of Liz's first marriage. Her marriage to Jonathan was short lived and he moved out in 1989. Liz Woodward and her son were last listed on the electoral roll in 1991.

By 1992 Apollo & Christine MULIRA had become the owners, and they still live in the house. He is a consultant at the Royal Worcester Group of Hospitals and they have four children - Joshua, Anthony, Charles and Anna. Apollo tells the story of how, as a Ugandan Doctor newly arrived in Winchester without a current passport, he had inadequate documentation to obtain a licence to marry Christine, a nurse at the same hospital. The bureaucrats ridiculed his suggestion that they should contact the Bishop. Eventually they did so, and were surprised when Bishop John Taylor was delighted to vouch for Apollo, whom he had baptised. The Bishop, when serving as a missionary, had been a friend of the Mulira family.

## No 33   STRENCLIFFE

The first occupant of this house, semi-detached from No 31 and a mirror image of it, was Mrs Eliza Elizabeth DEAKIN. In October 1910, from this address and described as a widow, she lent £550 to Messrs Baker & Warr, the builders of No 4, the loan being secured on that house. She was listed at *Strencliffe* in Kelly's Directories from 1912 to 1924 inclusive, and

---

[70] *Solihull News 2 November 2001*
[71] *Information from Mrs Anne Beal*
[72] *Information from Mrs Audrey Hall*
[73] *Information from Mrs Anne Beal*
[74] *Ibid*
[75] *Information from Roger & Ann Lucas*
[76] *GRO Index for Q/E December 1982 [Solihull S. 34 0061]*
[77] *Electoral Roll 1990*

in the electoral rolls until 1926. She had been born Eliza Wilkes in 1848[78] and had married Alfred Deakin in 1874[79]. The 1881 Census showed them at Rylands Farm, Coventry Road, Small Heath, with their daughters Ellen (aged 6) and Ada (2). Alfred, aged 35, employed 2 men and 2 boys. One of the latter, Thomas Taylor (15) from Yardley, who lived with the family, was described as 'a cowboy'. The farm was where the Singer factory now stands. A third daughter, Emma Elizabeth, was born in 1883[80]. The two elder daughters married the Dewbury brothers[81], whilst Emma married David Grey Davies. Alfred died, worth £1,223-9-6d, on 28 January 1903. His executors were his widow and elder daughters, Ellen & Ada. Eliza Deakin moved into *Strencliffe* with her mother Emma Wilkes, who lived with her until her death in 1917[82]. Eliza died aged 79 on 17 July 1927. Probate for her estate (£16,489-1-3d) was granted to her younger daughters Ada Dewbury and Emma Davies.

Ada had been born in 1879[83] and married William DEWBURY in 1918[84]. William had been born in 1876[85] and was recorded in the 1881 Census as the third son of John (timber & slate merchant) & Elizabeth Dewbury of 443 Coventry Road, Aston. William also became a timber merchant. He and Ada had one child, William Grey, known as Bill.

By 1932 William & Ada had installed a telephone (Solihull 0818, which remains the number today). Their servants changed frequently: in 1930/31 there was Estella Kathleen Mumford; in 1933/34 Anne Brazier; and in 1934/35 Elizabeth Selina Dorrell. The last named proved to have more staying power, and remained with the family until 1972. William died aged 68 on 6 September 1944. Probate for his estate, worth £10,007-7-3d, was granted to his widow and Lloyds Bank. Ada continued to live in the house with her son and daughter-in-law until she died aged 73 in 1952[86].

Bill DEWBURY was born in the house in 1921[87]. Educated at Eversfield School and then at Ellesmere, he served in the army in the war. Whilst in Greece he met Despina Denaxas and they married in 1948. They had a daughter Josephine born in 1950[88]. She married an Austrian and lives in Vienna. Bill became a civil engineer: now retired; he & Despina still live in the house today.

## No 35   THE BUNGALOW / ASHLEIGH HOUSE
'*A detached twin gabled house dating from about 1910. The gables are similar to those found at Nos 31 & 33: the brick gable projecting slightly forward of the timber gable which itself has a first floor jetty. This pair of gables are set off centre and emerge from a 'cat slide'*

---

[78] *GRO Index for Q/E March 1848 [Aston XVI 181]*
[79] *GRO Index for Q/E March 1874 [Aston 6d 335]*
[80] *GRO Index for Q/E June 1883 [Aston 6d 274]*
[81] *Information from Mr Bill Dewbury*
[82] *GRO Index for Q/E December 1917 [Meriden 6d 536]*
[83] *GRO Index for Q/E June 1879 [Aston 6d 265]*
[84] *GRO Index for September 1918 [Solihull 6d 1716]*
[85] *GRO Index for Q/E March 1876 [Aston 6d 330]*
[86] *GRO Index for Q/E Sept 1952 [Solihull 9c 710]*
[87] *GRO Index for Q/E June 1921 [Solihull 6d 1664]*
[88] *GRO Index for Q/E June 1950 [Birmingham 9c 293]*

*roof which is half hipped and sweeps down to first floor level in much the same way as Nos 23 & 25 and 27. This sweeping roof form seems to have been popular towards the end of the Edwardian era.'*[89].

Joseph Wells sold the land on which this house was built to John Arthur ROWLANDS in a conveyance dated 14 December 1907. Within three months the purchaser had to erect a good and substantial fence not less than five, nor more than seven feet high, on the back and southern boundaries.

John Rowlands was the son of Edward Rowlands, the senior partner of Rowlands & Co., Joseph Wells' solicitors, and the nephew of Hubert who succeeded his brother before the First World War. The 1881 Census had recorded John, aged 2, and his sister Winifred (5) at home in Homer Road, Solihull, with their parents Edward (31) & his wife Harriet (32). The family were still there in 1891 with both children attending school. John became an auctioneer and married Beatrice Annie Ryland on 2 June 1908 at St Mary, Acocks Green. She was the daughter of the late John Ryland, manufacturer, of Holmlea, Shirley Road, Acocks Green. The witnesses were the bride's brother John and the bridegroom's father Edward and brother Jacob[90].

Immediately after their marriage John & Beatrice came to live at No 35 which curiously, unless the house has been extended which seems improbable, they called *The Bungalow.* They lived here until 1927 and, from 1920 when it was built, looked across the road to No 32 which was indeed a bungalow. John & Beatrice never installed a telephone. They had a daughter, Winifred Amy, who was born in 1910 and never married. John Rowlands died in Birmingham General Hospital aged 75 and was buried on 9 March 1954 in St Alphege Churchyard. He shares a tombstone with his wife, who died in 1962, their daughter, who died on 11 March 1997, and his sister Winifred Chatterley who lived at No 7.

The first recording of the name change to *Ashleigh House* in the electoral rolls was in 1928 when Thomas & Annie Maud CROWLEY had come to live in the house. Mr Crowley, then of *Elan,* New Road, had purchased the property from John Rowlands probably at the same time (25 July 1927) as he bought the land to the south from Joseph Wells. This enabled the Crowleys to enlarge the garden and have a tennis court. But Mr Crowley sold the extra land on 27 November 1927 for the construction of No 37, apart from a strip 24 yards deep with a 2yd 1ft 6ins frontage to enable a garage to be built for *Ashleigh House.*

Born in 1867 in Birmingham, Thomas was the son of Thomas & Caroline Crowley. At the time of the 1881 Census he was one of twenty boarders at the Collegiate School, 9 Clarendon Place, Leamington, run by Arthur Riches and his sister, Ellen, with two teaching assistants and three servants. The 1901 Census showed the Crowley family at *Blythwood,* Blossomfield Road. The elder Thomas, aged 70, was a retired gold chain maker; the younger Thomas had become an insurance surveyor and he had three unmarried sisters, Eva aged 40, Bertha 31 and Elsie 22. Thomas left the house to marry in 1903, and at some point later the rest of the family moved to a house in Herbert Road which they also called *Blythwood.* The elder Thomas died there aged 95 on 7 January 1927 worth £42,022-8-2d, and Eva aged 74 on 22 November 1935 worth £10,445-5-1d. One of her executors was her brother Thomas,

---

[89] *Ashleigh Road Conservation Area by Simon Herrick*
[90] *Marriage Certificate*

described as 'of no occupation' - meaning that he had retired. Bertha moved to Boscombe and died there aged 73 on 24 April 1943 worth £18,384-19-1d. One of her executors was Edward Sutton Crowley, described as an insurance branch secretary.

At the age of 36, Thomas married Annie (aged a year younger) on 8 August 1903 at SS Mary & Bartholemew, Hampton-in-Arden[91]. Her father was Dr Ferdinand Page of *The Manor House* in the High Street, and her brother was called Eric. Eric was a surgeon in London who returned to Solihull to take over his father's practice when the latter was an old man. Thomas & Annie had two sons: Francis Sydney born in 1908[92] who appeared in the 1930 electoral roll, and Alfred Victor born on 11 August 1909 at *Arley Cottage*, New Road[93], who was listed in the 1931 electoral roll. One of the sons became a teacher, but his career was marred by breakdowns[94]. The Crowleys also had a servant, Ethel Chapman, in 1930-31. At some point Thomas and Annie moved to Shrewsbury, where Thomas died aged 82 on 20 November 1949 worth £12,201. His executors were his son Francis, and Edward Sutton Crowley.

By 1932[95] Horsley Kyle PATTERSON lived in the house. He had been recorded, aged two, in the 1881 Census with his parents, John James (35) and Agnes Knox (39) Patterson, younger brother and two sisters at 8 Noble Terrace, Gateshead. By 1891 Mrs Patterson was widowed and had moved with three sons (including Horsley, now at school aged 12) and a daughter to 24 Noble Terrace. Described as a manufacturer's manager[96], Horsley came from 7 Prospect Road, Moseley to take up residence at *Ashleigh House*. His first wife, whose maiden name was also Patterson and a relation of David Patterson of Widney Manor Road, had died early. Aged 52, he then married (Kathleen) Ruth Collins, a secretary aged 37, on 28 July 1931 at St Agnes, Moseley[97].

Horsley & Ruth had two sons - Kyle who died in Solihull Nursing Home on 6 June 1932 the day after he was born, and is commemorated on his parents' headstone in St Alphege Churchyard; and Jeremy David born in 1934. A violin/viola player in the Midland Youth Orchestra, Jeremy graduated from the Birmingham School of Music. He taught in both primary and secondary schools before his appointment as Senior Lecturer in Music Education at the City of Birmingham Polytechnic. Unmarried, he remained at home until he was 34[98]. He took early retirement in 1986. Jeremy conducted the Bromsgrove String Orchestra from 1966-72, and was appointed Music Director of the Birmingham Festival Choral Society in 1969, a position he still holds. He had adjudicated throughout the UK for every Choir of the Year Competition since its inception in 1984[99].

Horsley and Ruth installed a telephone (Solihull 0941) in *Ashleigh House*. They also

---

[91] *Marriage Certificate*
[92] *GRO Index for Q/E March 1908 [Solihull 6d 677]*
[93] *Birth Certificate*
[94] *Information from Mr Bill Dewbury*
[95] *Kelly's Directory for Warwickshire 1932*
[96] *Marriage Certificate*
[97] *Marriage Certificate*
[98] *Electoral Rolls 1955-68*
[99] *Birmingham Festival Choral Society Programme 25 November 2000*

painted much of the internal woodwork with bitumastic since Horsley worked for the Wales Bitumastic Company at the time[100]. Their servant was Louisa Jane Craddock in 1937 & 1938, who was replaced by Eve Dorothy Williscroft in 1939, but after the war they were no longer able to enjoy such a facility. Horsley died aged 73 on 11 January 1952. Probate for his estate (£35,342-2-11d) was granted to his widow and her sister Joyce Nancie Collins, spinster. Ruth continued to live in the house until her death aged 89 on 22 September 1982. Her estate amounted to £43,084. Horsley and Ruth share a grave in St Alphege Churchyard.

In 1983 Colin and Wendy GILL came to live in the house, with their children Rachel (born 1 July 1969) and Simon. The telephone number was 705 3621. Colin worked for Panasonic Microwaves[101]. The Gills stayed until 1995, when Colin & Diane HURT became the owners. They have Alex (born in 1996) and James (born in 1999).

## No 37   WENSLEY / ASHLEIGH LODGE

*Designed by John Burgess Surman in 1927, the house is fascinating because it represented the first real & successful departure from the Ashleigh Road norm. It breaks clear from any Edwardian influence and indeed looks forward to the bolder, 'modern' styles of the Thirties, which in the event never quite took off in Solihull. Not only is this house an important symbol of change, it is inherently interesting because of its single aspect design. This must have evolved from the client's brief which clearly demanded that as few rooms as possible look on to the street. This demand for privacy has been fully met. Although the obsession with privacy cannot be properly explained, one would expect the patron of this important and - for Solihull at least - radical house to be an enlightened man with more than a passing interest in architecture. Sure enough, the house was commissioned by Alfred Oxley who was Secretary to the Birmingham School of Art Committee at Margaret Street, Birmingham. It is quite possible that John Surman was remembered by Oxley as a student at the Birmingham School of Architecture which, at the time was part of the Margaret Street School of Art.*

*The house was built on a 6ins reinforced concrete raft which could have covered either poor ground or the rubble of a previous house. Although the Ordnance Survey of 1920 shows no house on the site, John Surman's drawing of 1927 notes that 'the present gates are to be refixed'. Therefore, there could have been a house on the site when Oxley bought it, but it would have endured an unusually short life.*

*The plans of the house show a 'Meal Room', 'Scullery' and so forth, but by now we have lost the 'China Pantry' of the earlier houses. All three bedrooms on the first floor face the garden and instead of windows to the street, the drawings show cupboards, bathroom, WC and a Box Room. John Surman has merely written 'Boxes'. The landscape was as thoroughly conceived as the house with carefully shaped borders arranged on a line of symmetry. Since the house was built, the garage has been carefully extended forward (and a large glass bow window added to the 'meal room'), with one or two associated internal alterations. The original drawings show a continuous string course around the house at 1st floor level, but this was not actually constructed. Apart from these variations, the front looks very much as*

[100] *Information from Mr Bill Dewbury*
[101] *Ibid*

*No 37 in 2002, designed by John Burgess Surman in 1927 and built on the garden and tennis court of No 35.*

*it did in 1928. Even the door, although unusual, is the original. Front windows serve only the living room and hall downstairs, and the first floor Boxes' room[102].*

Although Alfred Oxley commissioned the new house, and his initials appear over the fire place in the front room, he did not live there nor did he purchase the land. The latter was originally sold by Joseph Wells, the developer, for £330 on 25 July 1927 to Thomas CROWLEY of *Elan,* New Road, but soon to be of *Ashleigh House* (No 35). The tennis court of the latter house was on this plot, which had a frontage of 20yds 1ft 6ins and an overall area of 1650 sq yds.

Within four months, on 27 November 1927, Mr Crowley sold the land, but with a frontage reduced to 18 yards, for £357-15s to William Edward Allen OXLEY, possibly Alfred's nephew, of *The Pont,* Wood End, Tanworth-in-Arden. The area of the land was now 1590 sq yds because a strip 24 yards deep by 2yds 1ft 6ins had been retained by *Ashleigh House,* presumably for an extension. A condition in the conveyance was that only one detached house should be erected, '*such house to be of the set first cost of £1,000 at the least'.* John Surman's plans were approved by Solihull Rural District Council on 14 February 1928. The building contract was let to Charles J.Grove & Sons of Dorridge who reported on 26 March that the foundations were ready for inspection, and on 15 September that the house was ready for occupation.

---

[102] *Ashleigh Road Conservation Area by Simon Herrick*

The 1929 electoral roll showed that William Oxley had taken up residence and named his house *Wensley*. But the name was rarely used and even when Mr Oxley mortgaged the property for £1,000 (at 5% interest) on 7 July 1928 to Birmingham Incorporated Building Society, it was referred to as No 37. Described as a municipal servant in the conveyances, William succeeded Alfred Oxley as the Secretary of the Birmingham School of Art. He had been born on 29 April 1883 at Helmsley, Yorkshire, the son of Charles and Mary Adah Oxley nee Wood[103]. He lived alone at *Wensley* until 1932, and never installed a telephone. When he died, aged 59, in Birmingham General Hospital on 22 May 1942, he was described as 'of *Ashgrove,* Toddington, Cheltenham and The College of Arts & Crafts, Margaret Street, Birmingham'. Barclays Bank was the executor of his £8,077-0-7d estate.

On 21 February 1933 (Archibald) Michael FLETCHER, art master, of 15 Beechwood Road, Warley Woods, Birmingham, bought the property for £1,500. On the following day he raised a mortgage with the Dudley & District Benefit Building Society for £1,200 at an interest rate of 4.5%. Repayments were to be made weekly at £2; the mortgage was paid off on 16 November 1943. Michael and his wife, Lily Gwendoline, did not have a telephone in 1935, nor any living-in servants. On 18 November 1942 he sold the property to his wife for the same sum as he originally had paid for it; the witness being their next door neighbour, Horsley K. Patterson. Michael & Lily made their wills on 31 October 1949, each appointing Lloyds Bank as their executor. Mrs Fletcher died aged 65 on 20 April 1955 worth £12,238-18-2d, and was buried in St Alphege Churchyard on 22 April[104]. Michael became the owner of the house once again, and had Emeline Watkins as a housekeeper in 1956 and Winifred Searle in 1957. The telephone number in 1955 was Solihull 0787, and this remained the number at least until 1983. Michael died aged 69 on 10 August 1957 at The Accident Hospital, Birmingham[105], and was buried on 15 August[106], sharing a gravestone with his wife in St Alphege Churchyard. His estate amounted to £13,454-11-7d.

Howard Thompson BLENCH of *Blythe Prior,* Wootton Lane, Berkswell bought the property on 7 November 1957 for £5,000. His wife was called Patricia and they stayed for nine years. Philip Brian and Dora Eleanor COLLINS of 225 Blossomfield Road became the owners on 6 May 1966. They bought for £9,750 and sold on 20 October 1969 for £11,250. The purchasers were Thomas Douglas and Joan Eileen Justham RUSSELL of 266 Brooklands Road, Manchester. They had two children David and Pamela (the latter born 27 March 1953). Faulkner Mitchell lived with them in 1975, and both the children had left by the following year.

By 1978 William A. and Joan S. GARDNER had arrived. Their son William was 18 on 14 January 1979, and their daughter Fiona was 18 on 21 May 1982. They retained the 0787 telephone number. The Gardners, who extended the garage so carefully, left in 1983. They were replaced by Neil & Linda TIBBATTS, who did not stay long. He was an interior designer. Roy & Margaret BOULTER (1989-91) obtained planning permission on

---

[103] *Birth Certificate*
[104] *Burial Records of St Alphege Church*
[105] *Probate Index of Wills*
[106] *Burial Records of St Alphege Church*

*No 37a in 2002. It was built in 1967 on the tennis court of No 39, typical of small, detached houses of the period in Solihull.*

11 January 1990 for a two storey garden store and en suite bathroom above on the south side of the house, and a (further) garage extension, but this was never built. Dr Jonathan & Roslyn DUCKETT were shown in the electoral rolls between 1992-94 when their marriage broke down. Roslyn, a physiotherapist, continued to live in the house, reverting to her maiden name of WHEELER. Andrew & Mary WESTLEY, who kindly loaned the deeds of their house, have lived there since 1995. They have restored the rear garden, at the bottom of which is an Anderson Shelter from the Second World War.

### No 37a  RYLANDS
This house was built in 1967 by the developer Leonard SHEPHERD of Manor Road, on the tennis court that had originally belonged to No 39. The first occupants were Alfred and Florence MAYHEW[107], who stayed until 1982. Horace and Irene HUMPHRIES, initially with Robert W Humphries, had arrived by 1984[108] and remained until 1992

The owner from then until 1996 was Winifred BURROWS. She was then succeeded by William F. and Doris J.SMITH, who remain the current occupants.

---

[107] *Electoral Roll 1968*
[108] *Electoral Roll 1984*

**No 39   HARBLE DOWN**

Guarding the southern entrance to Ashleigh Road, this substantial house stands on a somewhat exposed site which was even more open originally as Nos 37 & 37A were not built until 1927 & 1976 respectively. Moreover for its first twenty years it was the sole postern to the road as the western side remained undeveloped until the early 1920s.

The plot was sold by Joseph Albert Wells, the developer of the road, of Newtown Row, Birmingham on 6 November 1905 for £350 to John Henry HOLLAND, pin manufacturer, of *Rosendale*, Oxford Road, Moseley. It had a 24 yard frontage to Ashleigh Road, the standard depth of 80yd 1ft 6ins, and a width of 31 yards at the rear, along which there was a 9ft wide party passage leading northwards from Streetsbrook Road. The area of the plot was 2200 sq yds (or thereabouts, as the conveyance qualified this figure). The fields on the other side of the passage belonged to R.S.Chattock, whilst the land to the north of the plot was still in the vendor's ownership. The purchaser, within three months, had to erect a fence no less than 5ft, nor more than 7ft, high on the east & north sides; and also level & construct the party passage, and maintain this in good condition. The building line was 10 yards back from both Ashleigh Road & Streetsbrook Road.

John HOLLAND lost no time in building his house, which he called *Harble Down*, as he appeared on the 1908 Electoral Roll. He was described as a retired steel pin manufacturer, but curiously still of *Rosendale*, Oxford Road, Moseley, when he sold *Harble Down* on 30 March 1916 for £1,000.

The purchaser was John Henry THORLEY, works manager, of 28 Hatfield Road, Handsworth. Mr Thorley added to the property by buying from Mr Wells, the developer, on 15 October 1920 for £256-11-10d the land to the north. This had a frontage of 17 yards to Ashleigh Road and the standard depth, ie an area of 1368 sq yds (or thereabouts). The party passage seems to have disappeared. John Thorley had been born in 1878[109] and was listed in the 1881 Census living with his grandfather, Frederick Pearson, a lithographic printer aged 48, and the latter's wife and family at 81 Summer Road, Edgbaston. John married Lizzie Janet Merridew on 26 December 1902 at St Bartholemew, Edgbaston. Aged 23, a year younger than John, she was the daughter of William Merridew who was described as a manager[110]. They had at least one child - Edwin Frederick born in 1904[111] who was listed in the 1928 electoral roll after the family had moved to *Kidlington*, The Crescent. Later John and Lizzie moved to *The Spinney,* Crickley Hill, Witcombe, Cheltenham. John died on 8 September 1950 at The Royal Victoria & West Hampshire Hospital, Boscombe. Probate for his estate (£1,925-10-11d) was granted to his widow.

Louisa Jane GRIFFITHS, the wife of Alfred GRIFFITHS, glass manufacturer & merchant, of *Elsmore*, Lyttleton Road, Stetchford bought the enlarged property on 29 June 1926 for £2,620 from Mr Thorley. It had a 41 yard frontage to Ashleigh Road, a depth of 80yd 1ft 6ins and an eastern boundary of 48 yards, making an area of 3568 sq yds. A mortgage for an undisclosed sum appears to have been obtained from St Philip's Building Society. Nearly a year later - on 28 April 1927 - Mrs Griffiths sold a small irregularly shaped

---

[109] *GRO Index for Q/E June 1878 [Birmingham 6d 82]*
[110] *Marriage Certificate*
[111] *GRO Index for Q/E September 1904 [West Bromwich 6b 855]*

strip of land, never more than 3.5ft wide, along the eastern boundary to Thomas Henry Restall of *Maybank,* Streetsbrook Road, her neighbour.

The Griffiths had a telephone (Solihull 411) by 1928[112], which - with the introduction of four figure numbers in 1931 - became 0411. By this date also the name of the house had become one word. The May 1929 electoral roll listed Winifred Annie Mills, presumably a servant, also living at *Harbledown*, but she had disappeared by October 1930. The Griffiths had two sons, Alfred Frederick and Thomas William, both of whom became glass merchants[113]. Thomas was born in 1908[114] and was shown on the electoral register at home from 1930 to 1935, when the family were joined by Winifred Stringer (presumably a servant). On 2 June 1932 Mr & Mrs Griffiths took out a mortgage for £1,500 with Lloyds Bank (interest rate undisclosed), which was redeemed on 29 May 1940, the day before Louisa - now widowed - sold the property. Alfred had died aged 74 on 15 January 1940, worth £3,245-11-5d.

Henry Albert Frederick ELLINGHOUSE, company director, of *Gowan Lea,* Meriden Road, Hampton-in-Arden bought *Harbledown* on 30 May 1940 for £1,800. The sharp drop in price was presumably a reflection of low property values nine months into the war. On the same day Mr Ellinghouse mortgaged the property for £1,250 with The Coventry & District Permanent Money Society. The interest rate was 6.5% pa. The mortgage was redeemed on 26 July 1947. Henry Ellinghouses's wife was called Elizabeth[115], and they had a servant - Eileen Martin in 1945-7, replaced by Margaret Thompson from 1948. The telephone number was Solihull 1044, but the subscriber's name was listed as Frederick Ellinghouse.

The next owner was Millicent Joan WOODFIELD (nee Burman), the wife of Alfred Woodfield of 47 Danford Lane, Solihull, who bought the property on 25 January 1949 for £4,500. The telephone number was now Solihull 0835. Mr Woodfield was a merchant banker with Hambros[116]. They had a daughter called Josephine, born in 1937[117], who married Charles Warden in 1962[118] and now lives in Hatton Park; and a son Christopher[119] who married Rosemary J.Willetts in 1965[120]. The Woodfields stayed 15 years before moving out to *Up Orchard,* Kings Lane, Snitterfield. Mrs Woodfield sold No 39 on 21 December 1964 for £12,250 to L.G.SHEPHERD Ltd of 54 Manor Road, Solihull.

Leonard Shepherd described his company as builders, but he was more interested in property development. Solihull Council refused permission on 28 November 1963 for the erection of 3 storey luxury flats on the site, and on 3 July 1964 for 20 flats & 20 garages, so Mr Shepherd broke up the property. Half (40 yards) of the original depth of the site, with its valuable frontage to Streetsbrook Road, was sold; as was the additional land to the north

[112] *Kelly's Directory for Warwickshire 1928*
[113] *Probate Index of Wills*
[114] *GRO Index for Q/E September 1908 [Solihull 6d 625]*
[115] *Electoral Roll 1945*
[116] *Information from Mrs Josephine Warden (nee Woodfield)*
[117] *GRO Index for Q/E December 1937 [Birmingham 6d 495]*
[118] *GRO Index for Q/E September 1962 [Solihull 9c 2688]*
[119] *Electoral Roll 1962*
[120] *GRO Index for Q/E March 1965 [Warwick 9c 2858]*

which John Thorley had acquired in 1920, and on which No 37A now stands, in place of the tennis court[121].

The remaining emasculated plot, with No 39 upon it, was bought on 22 January 1965 for £6,250 by Vera Marjorie HOARE (nee Prosser), the wife of Cyril Albert Hoare, director of a wholesale flour company[122], of 91 Stratford Road, Shirley. Under the terms of the conveyance Mrs Hoare had to fence her land. On the same day she mortgaged the property to Lloyds Bank: neither the amount raised, nor the interest rate, were stated in the document. The Hoares sought planning permission on 8 May 1972 for the construction of a porch, the alteration of the breakfast room window, and the conversion of an outbuilding into a study & a new WC. The plans were drawn up by M.J.Timings, architectural technician, of 18 Halfcot Avenue, Pedmore, Stourbridge. Approval was given on 12 July 1972.

Vera Prosser had married Cyril Hoare in 1939[123]. They had four children: Michael C. born in 1943[124], Christine W. born in 1947[125], Terence J. born in 1951[126], and Ivan born on 17 October 1958. In 1967[127] they also adopted a boy of mixed parentage - Colin Andrew - who had been born in 1966. The Hoare's telephone number was 705 6970. On leaving Solihull they went to the Isle of Wight[128].

Mrs Hoare sold the house on 25 October 1979 to Richard & Helen BIRD, the present owners, who kindly lent the property deeds to provide the basis of the above information. They moved from Hampton Lane, bringing their telephone number (705 4684) with them. Sir Richard Geoffrey Chapman Bird, born on 3 November 1935, is the 4th Baronet, the grandson of Sir Alfred Bird who conveyed Tudor Grange to the Borough of Solihull for recreational & educational purposes. Richard married, first, Gillian Frances Haggett of Solihull in 1957 and had Rowena, three further daughters, as well as John Andrew (born 19 January 1964) and Mark (born 27 September 1965). Gillian died in 1966. Richard married secondly in 1968 Helen Patricia Beaumont of Pontefract. They have Catherine (born 13 January 1970) and Denise (born 6 April 1972)[129].

---

[121] *Information from Mrs Josephine Warden (nee Woodfield)*

[122] *Information from Ann & Roger Lucas*

[123] *GRO Index for Q/E September 1939 [Birmingham 6d 578]*

[124] *GRO Index for Q/E September 1943 [Birmingham 6d 603]*

[125] *GRO Index for Q/E June 1947 [Birmingham 9c 825]*

[126] *GRO Index for Q/E March 1951 [Birmingham 9c 460]*

[127] *Adoption reference 00007 631*

[128] *Information from Roger & Ann Lucas*

[129] *Who's Who 2001*

# 8. APPENDICES

**I    Disposals by J.A.Wells**

following his acquisition of the land on 10 March 1903 for £3,526-15s.

| **Land only:** Date | | | **Number** | **Price** | **Frontage** |
|---|---|---|---|---|---|
| 17 | October | 1903 | 12 | £273-14s | 24 yards |
| 8 | July | 1904 | 20 | £309-12s | 26 yards |
| 10 | March | 1904 | 15 & 17 | £225 | 19 yards |
| 23 | December | 1904 | 19 | £225 | 19 yards |
| 2 | October | 1905 | 14, 16 & 18 | £500 | 42 yards |
| 6 | November | 1905 | 39 | £350 | 24 yards |
| 29 | September | 1906 | 21 | £350 | 24 yds 2ft |
| 21 | February | 1907 | 4 | £211-6-3d | 15 yards |
| 13 | July | 1909 | 30 | £225-8s | 16 yards |
| 25 | July | 1927 | 37 | £330 | 20 yds 1.5ft |
| **Land with house built thereon.** | | | | | |
| 24 | June | 1911 | 7 & 9 | £2,000 (the pair) | Each 11yds 9ins |
| 24 | June | 1911 | 11 & 13 | £2,000 (the pair) | Each 11yds 9ins |
| 24 | June | 1911 | 2 | £1,012-10s | 15 yards |
| 8 | May | 1920 | 3 | £1,750 | 16yds 1ft 6ins |

Analysis of the land only transactions shows that for the first sale in 1903 Mr Wells charged £11.40 per yard of frontage. In the next three sales in 1904 the cost rose slightly to £11.90, but for No 39 in 1905 he charged £14.60 per yard. This reduced to £14.20 for No 21, and both later sales were at the rate of £14.10 per yard.

## II   The Dutfields of No 14.

JAMES PHILIP POUND DUTFIELD was a successful coal merchant, who founded the Birmingham Citizens Permanent Building Society and was a prominent freemason.

He was born on 15 December 1858 at Lander Street, Saltley[1], the eldest son of James & Ann Dutfield. The 1881 Census recorded the Dutfields at Clive Place, Arthur Road, Aston. James the father, aged 52, was a store clerk at the Gas Works and had originally come from Cotheridge (Worcs). His wife (48) had been born in Worcester. Their son James (22) was a wages clerk at the gas works; Charlotte (19) was a dressmaker; William (14) a 'shop boy at Druggist shop'; whilst Ada (12) & George (9) were still at school.

James married Mary Jane Cope at St Peter the Great, Worcester on 28 April 1884. Both gave their age as 25; Mary had been born in 1859[2]. The Cope family were recorded in the 1881 Census at 57 Conybere Street, Aston[3]. Thomas Cope, a silversmith aged 52, and his wife Elizabeth 51 had both been born in Birmingham, as had her father Joseph Parker a gardener of 75 who lived with them. There were 6 children, all unmarried, namely: Joseph 29 an unemployed brassfounder; Emma 24 a draper's assistant born, like all her younger siblings, at Kings Norton (Worcestershire); Mary Jane 22 a brush drawer; Thomas 17 a chaser in brass; William 14 a clerk (accountant); and Alice 12 at school. Alice signed as a witness at Mary's marriage.

On his marriage certificate James described himself as a coal merchant. This was the occupation he pursued for the rest of his life, and how he was described in 1905 when buying the plot of land in Ashleigh Road; and in the Birmingham 1911 telephone directory when he had his office at 14 Temple Street. It was through this occupation that he came to know the Chamberlain family, and also developed his other interests. In 1890, at the age of 31, he founded the Birmingham Citizens Permanent Building Society, of which he was Managing Director & Secretary until the time of his death. This enabled him to move house frequently. He was active, with Joseph Chamberlain, in the formation of the Liberal Unionist Party, and was a prominent freemason.

In 1887 James and Mary were living in Havelock Road, Saltley, but by the time of the 1891 Census (Sunday 5 April) they had moved to Highfield Road, Saltley[4] with their three eldest children, the youngest of whom had only just been born. In all they had four children, Sydney, Lilian, Amy and Dora. By 1893 they were at 152 Alum Rock, Saltley.[5] Unfortunately Mary died on 15 February 1899 in their home at 40 Charles Road, Bordesley[6], after only 15 years of marriage.

After Mary's death, James (now aged 41) married Constance Lizzie Aldridge (31), known as Connie, at St Matthew, Salford Priors on 18 January 1900[7]. His daughter Lilian

---

[1] *Birth Certificate*
[2] *GRO Index for Q/E March 1859 [Kings Norton 6c 431]*
[3] *Public Record Office, RG11 3015 14*
[4] *Public Record Office, RG12 2427 76*
[5] *Dora's Birth Certificate*
[6] *Probate Index of Wills*
[7] *Marriage Certificate*

was one of the witnesses. Connie had become his cook/housekeeper after Mary's death. She was the daughter of Thomas Clements Aldridge (1837/8 - 1914), the schoolmaster of Perkins Free School, Evesham Road, Salford Priors (in Warwickshire, although only 6 miles from Evesham). Thomas' second wife was his assistant at the school where they lived at the time of the 1881 Census[8] with three children from Thomas' first marriage to Eliza Cook - Henry Clements aged 13, Connie, and Gertrude Helena (10) all born at Salford Priors.

James & Connie, and James' children from his first marriage, lived at 40 Charles Road, Bordesley at the time of the 1901 Census. Gertrude Goodman, aged 16, was their domestic servant. The Dutfield family moved into the newly built house in Ashleigh Road, Solihull as soon as it was finished in 1905/6 and stayed until 1916. James died at his home Wood Lawn, Station Road, Balsall Common, on 18 December 1943, leaving an estate of £11,840 for which probate was granted to The Midland Bank. *The Birmingham Post* carried his obituary on Christmas Eve: *James Dutfield was the Managing Director & Secretary of the Birmingham Citizens Permanent Building Society which he founded 53 years ago. He was a prominent freemason and was for some years honorary secretary of the Masonic Peace Memorial Temple in Broad Street. In his early years he was an active worker at the formation of the Liberal Unionist Party in which he was closely associated with Joseph Chamberlain. He was 85 and leaves a widow, one son and three daughters.*

Connie moved to 15 Stivichall Croft, Coventry and died aged 89 on 8 February 1958 at 1 Morningside, Coventry. The executors for her estate (£34,769-1-5d) were Harry Dean, machine tool representative; Norman Scott, cement manufacturer; and Arthur Jagger, solicitor.'

By his first marriage with Mary Cope, James had four children:

**Sydney James**: born in 1885[10], he was listed in the 1891 Census but, unusually for a 6 year old, was not described as a scholar. In the 1901 Census his occupation was given as 'CC Clerk, factory worker'. He had attended Saltley Training College, and joined the Birmingham Citizens Permanent Building Society in 1902. In 1931 he was appointed Assistant Secretary, and in 1944 he succeeded his father as Manager & Secretary, ie Chief Executive. He retired in March 1950. As a young man he had served for five years in the Shropshire Yeomanry, becoming an NCO; and like his father he was a zealous freemason[11]. He bought a cottage next to The Bell Inn in Salford Priors as a holiday home, which was very convenient as he was a heavy drinker[12].

He married, first, Minnie E. Lloyd in 1914[13]. Sadly she died aged only 33 in 1925[14]. Secondly Sydney married Ethel Thompson, who worked for Cadburys, in 1943[15]. He died aged 66 at his home, 956 Bristol Road, Selly Oak, in 1951[16].

---

[8] *Public Record Office, RG11 3109 62*
[9] *Probate Index of Wills*
[10] *GRO Index for Q/E June 1885 [Aston 6d 212]*
[11] *Obituary in The Birmingham Post*
[12] *Information from Mrs Sheila Gilbert (nee Dean)*
[13] *GRO Index for Q/E June 1914 [West Bromwich 6b 1635]*
[14] *GRO Index for Q/E March 1925 [Solihull 6d 899]*
[15] *GRO Index for Q/E June 1943 [Birmingham 6d 958]*
[16] *GRO Index for Q/E December 1951 [Birmingham 9c 452]*

**Lilian May**: born on 1 June 1887 at Clifton House, Havelock Road, Saltley[17], she was listed in the 1891 Census aged 3. In 1901 her age was given as 12. After the death of her mother in 1899, she had been sent to boarding school in Norwich but was brought home (and her education effectively finished) at the age of 13 soon after her father remarried. When the First World War started she persuaded her father to allow her to help at the first Southern General Hospital in Birmingham (now the City Hospital). After the war she trained and qualified as a nurse at the Coventry & Warwickshire Hospital[18]. She married Harry Archibald Dean, an engineer at Alfred Herberts, in 1920[19]. They had Sheila, born in 1926[20], who married Peter Gilbert, an architect (died 1998) and had two sons. Lilian died aged 99 on 20 February 1987.

**Amy Ethel:** was born on 28 March 1891 at Linwood House, Highfield Road, Saltley, her mother informing the Registrar on 8 May[21]. In the Census she was called Madge, presumably an early pet name, and her age was given as 3 weeks, when in fact she was only a week old. Aged 10 in 1901 Census, her occupation, like that of her sisters, was unrecorded. Like her elder sister, she had been sent to boarding school but brought home after her father remarried. She herself married John A. Wright in 1923[22]. Though born in England, he had spent time in Canada and it was there that they went to live. They had a son, David. Amy died aged 68 in Vancouver in 1961. David is a frequent visitor with his wife to England.

**Dora Janet:** was born on 25 November 1893 at 152 Alum Rock Road, Saltley, her mother informing the Registrar on 1 January 1894[23]. She appeared in the 1901 Census aged 7. She lived with her father and step-mother for many years, and made use of her father's position in the building society to buy or build residential property, eg with Mason's the builders at Balsall Common[24]. At the age of 48 she married Norman Scott in 1942[25]. She died on 19 January 1990.

---

[17] *Birth Certificate*
[18] *Information from Mrs Sheila Gilbert (nee Dean)*
[19] *GRO Index for Q/E September 1920 [Kings Norton 6d 581]*
[20] *GRO Index for Q/E September 1926 [Coventry 6d 1211]*
[21] *Birth Certificate*
[22] *GRO Index for Q/E September 1923 [Kings Norton 6d 281]*
[23] *Birth Certificate*
[24] *Information from Mrs Sheila Gilbert (nee Dean)*
[25] *GRO Index for Q/E March 1942 [Meriden 6d 1508]*

### III The Family of Hugh Aldis of No 16

Hugh ALDIS lived at No 16 from 1918-1938. His father was James Arthur Aldis who had been born in London on 7 February 1842, the son of the Revd. John Aldis, a noted Baptist minister. James was educated at the City of London School and then went up to Trinity College Cambridge as a Sizar[26] in 1859. He graduated as 6th Wrangler[27] in 1863 and took his MA three years later. He was the Headmaster of La Martiniere, Calcutta, 1868-75 and then returned to England, where he became an assistant master at Dulwich College 1876-78. The 1881 Census listed James (aged 39) & his wife Frances (34) with their family at 53 Lichfield Street, Walsall. Besides Hugh (10), they had twins Maud & Ethel (7), and Edith (6) all born in Bengal (ie Calcutta), Arthur (2), and Norah (1). Louisa Davies (19) was nursemaid for the children & Mrs Jane Boxall (37) was their cook. James was the Second Master at Queen Mary's College, Walsall 1879-80, and then became its Head Master 1881-97. He celebrated his diamond wedding to Frances Emily WEBB on 15 June 1929 when they were living at Dunwich, Suffolk. She died there on 30 August 1932, and he on 6 December 1935, aged 93[28].

James' elder brother (and Hugh's uncle) was William Steadman Aldis (10 February 1839 - 7 March 1928). Born at Southwark, the second son of the Revd. John Aldis, William was educated at the City of London School (1851-57) and Trinity College, Cambridge, where he graduated in 1861 as Senior Wrangler and first Smith's Prizeman. His success was indirectly of public importance. At that time no one could take a Fellowship in any college without signing a declaration that he was a *bona fide* member of the Church of England. For 13 years (1847-59) Trinity College had failed to secure a Senior Wrangler. In 1860 they had Stirling, afterwards Lord Justice, but he - being a United Presbyterian - refused to sign the declaration, and in 1861 William Aldis, a Baptist like most of his family, made the same refusal. These events, coupled with the subsequent conspicuous successes of William's two younger brothers, set on foot an agitation which ended the religious disabilities at both Oxford & Cambridge.

For a decade after his graduation William Aldis worked as a private tutor in mathematics in Cambridge. He and his wife were leading advocates for the admission of women to examinations and degrees in the University, and drew up a petition which was extensively signed throughout the Kingdom. The outcome of this movement was that women were allowed after 1897 to compete in the Tripos Examinations on the same terms as men, and the results were published in the University Calendar.

In 1870 William was appointed Professor of Mathematics, and later Principal of the College of Science, at Newcastle-on-Tyne. He was well read in the literature of five languages, speaking French & German fluently, and whilst at Newcastle added Hebrew.

---

[26] *The holder of a scholarship*

[27] *The term applied in the University of Cambridge for one who has obtained first class honours in Part II (ie the final exam) of the mathematical tripos. The first man was (until 1909) called the Senior Wrangler. A wrangler is a disputant, and the name arises from the former public disputations in which candidates were required to take part.*

[28] *Alumni Cantabrigensis 1752-1900 by J.A.Venn. CUP 1940*

The result was that the Newcastle Professor of Mathematics was sometimes employed by the University of Durham to examine divinity students in Hebrew[29]. In 1883 he was appointed Professor of Mathematics at Auckland University in New Zealand, where he remained until his retirement and return to England in 1897. William Aldis was remarkable not only for his mathematical attainments (his 'Solid Geometry' and 'Optics' long remained standard works), but also for his wide general knowledge, religious faith, interest in social and political reforms and lovable disposition. William married Mary, eldest daughter of the Revd William Robinson the well known Minister of St Andrew's Street Chapel, Cambridge, and had a son & two daughters[30].

James' other younger brother was Thomas Steadman Aldis who was born on 6 August 1843. Like his brothers he went to the City of London School (1854-62) and Trinity College, Cambridge where he graduated in mathematics in 1866 as 2nd Wrangler. He took his MA in 1869 and became an Inspector of Schools in 1872. He was promoted Chief Divisional Inspector in 1898. He resided latterly at Bowhayes, Bridport and died on 25 September 1908 at Bournemouth with an obituary in The Times on 29 September.

Finally, Hugh's brother was Arthur Cyril Webb Aldis. Born in 1879, he was educated at King Edward School, Birmingham and Trinity Hall, Cambridge. He was the 23rd Wrangler in 1900 and was appointed Fellow of his College 1901-08. He joined his brother as the junior partner in Aldis Brothers of Sparkhill[31]. He lived at Craig-y-Don, Dorridge, from 1916 until at least 1936[32].

**Postscript**

This history represents the results of considerable research over several years, combined with information given to me by present and past residents. It is inevitably more detailed about some houses than others, there may be some inaccuracies, and changes occur as people move on and newcomers arrive. History has no beginning and no end. If any readers have more information to add, it would be welcome.

---

[29] *Source: biography by his eldest daughter*
[30] *The Times obituary 13 March 1928*
[31] *Alumni Cantabrigensis 1752-1900 by J.A.Venn. CUP 1940*
[32] *Kelly's Directory for Warwickshire 1936*

## IV Genealogical tree of the Lancaster family

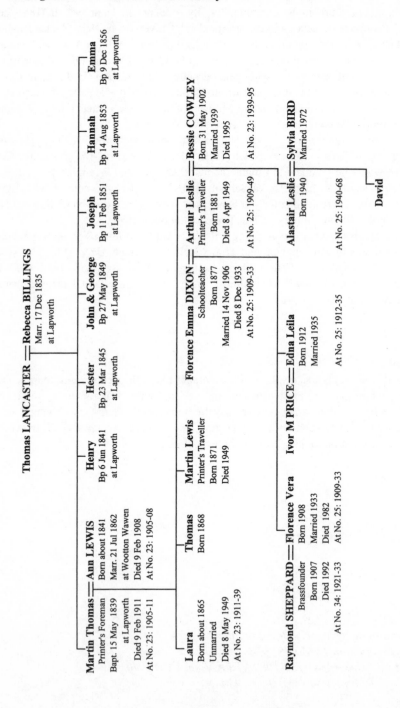

## V   List of Illustrations with Sources

Page

**Key:** AC – Angela Cameron, AG – Angus Gray, AS – Andrew Spittle, BL – Birmingham Central Library, CA – Conservation Area Book, DM – Roads of Solihull by Donovan Moore, MY – Maureen Yardley, OS – Ordnance Survey, RO – Warwick County Record Office, SG – Sheila Gilbert, SH – Simon Herrick, SL – Solihull Library.

# 9. INDEX